Fuchsias

for greenhouse and garden

3801.
Pub. by S. Curtis, Glazenwood, Essex, June 1. 1840.
Swan Sc.

Fuchsias
for greenhouse and garden

David Clark

Series editor John Simmons
OBE, VMH

The Royal Botanic Gardens, Kew
in association with

AURA BOOKS plc

First published in 1987. This edition published in 1991 by
The Hamlyn Publishing Group Limited,
part of Reed International Books, Michelin House, 81 Fulham Road,
London SW3 6RB.

ISBN 0 600 57258 7

Filmset in England by Vision Typesetting, Manchester
in 11 on 12 pt Bembo

Produced by Mandarin Offset.
Printed in Hong Kong.

Contents

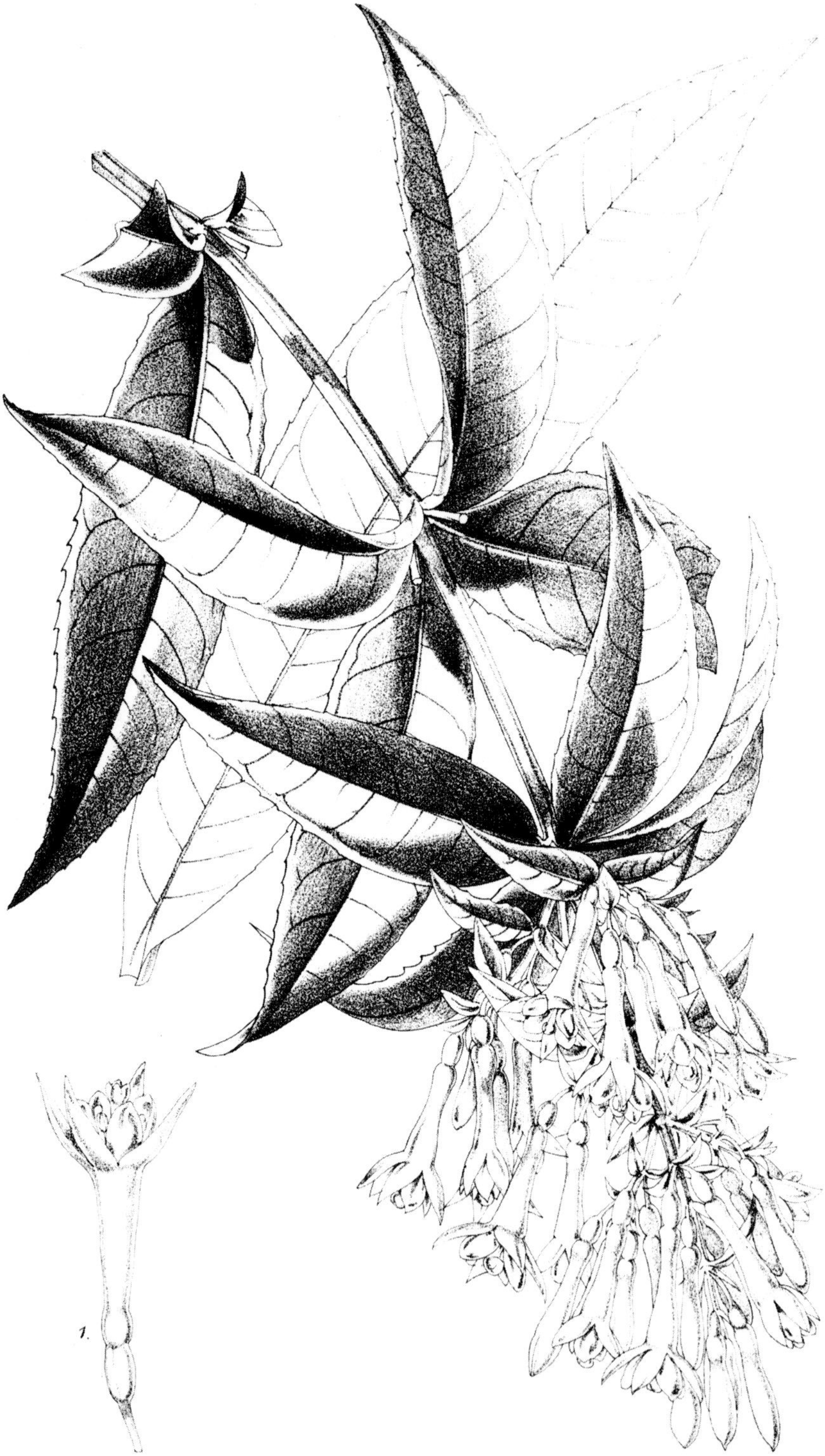

1.

W. Fitch, del et lith.

Vincent Brooks, Day & Son, Imp.

Preface

The Royal Botanic Gardens, Kew with their herbarium, library, laboratories and unrivalled collection of living plants, form one of the world's most important centres of botanical science. Their origins, however, can be traced back to a modest nine-acre site in the Pleasure Garden at Kew which Augusta, the Dowager Princess of Wales and mother of King George III, set aside for the cultivation of new and interesting plants.

On this site were grown many of the exotic species which reached England for the first time during this period of mercantile and colonial expansion. Trees such as our oldest specimens of *Sophora japonica* from China and *Robinia pseudoacacia* from America were planted for the Princess and still flourish at Kew, as do many accessions from Africa and Australia.

Many of Kew's earliest collectors were botanical explorers who made difficult and dangerous journeys to remote and unknown parts of the world in their search for economically important or beautiful plants. The work of Kew's botanists in gathering new species was complemented by that of Kew's gardeners, who were responsible for their care and propagation. The gardeners were also responsible for trans-shipping living plants from Kew to other parts of the world, and the Gardens rapidly became a clearing house through which 'useful' species grown in one continent were transferred to another.

At the present time, the living collections of the Royal Botanic Gardens contain approximately 50,000 types of flowering plants from every corner of the earth. Such a collection makes unending demands on the skills and dedication of those entrusted with its care. It also provides an unrivalled opportunity for gardening staff to familiarize themselves with the diverse requirements of plants from the many different climatic and geological regions of the world. The plants in the Royal Botanic Gardens are no museum collection, however. As in the eighteenth and nineteenth centuries, the Gardens continue to distribute living plant material on a worldwide basis, though they now use modern facilities such as the micropropagation unit at Kew and the Seed Bank at Wakehurst Place. The Gardens are also actively involved in the conservation of the world's plant resources and in supplying scientists at Kew and elsewhere with the plants and plant material required for their research. This may range from basic studies of the ways in which plants have evolved to the isolation of plant chemicals of potential use in agriculture and medicine. Whatever the purpose of the research, there is inevitably a need to grow plants and to grow them well, whether they be plants from the rain forests of the Amazon or from the deserts of Africa.

Your interest in gardening may be neither scientific nor economic, but I believe that the expert advice provided by specialist authors in this new series of *Kew Gardening Guides* will provide help of a quality that can be given only by gardeners with long experience of the art and science of cultivating a particular group of plants.

E. Arthur Bell
Director, Royal Botanic Gardens, Kew

Opposite: *Fuchsia sessilifolia*

Foreword

Gardening is in part instinctive, in part experience. Look in any village or town and you will see many gardens, balconies or even windowsills full of healthy plants brightening up the streets. However, there are always likely to be other plots that are sterile and devoid of plants, or overgrown and unloved. Admittedly gardening is laborious, but the hours spent sweating behind a mower on a hot summer's day will be amply rewarded when the smooth green lawn is admired; the painful nettle stings incurred while clearing ground will soon be forgotten when the buds of newly planted shrubs burst forth in spring.

These few examples of the joy and pain of gardening are all part of its attraction to its devotees. The successful gardeners and plant lovers of this world come to understand plants instinctively, learning their likes and dislikes, their lifespan and ultimate size, recognizing and correcting ailments before they become serious. They work with the seasons of the year, not against them; they think ahead, driven by caring, being aware of when conditions are right for planting, mowing or harvesting and, perhaps most important of all, they know when to leave well alone.

This understanding of the natural order cannot be learned overnight. It is a continuous two-way process that lasts a lifetime. In creating a garden, past masters such as Humphry Repton in the eighteenth century or Gertrude Jekyll in the nineteenth perceived and enhanced the natural advantages of a site, and Jekyll in particular was an acute observer of the countryside and its seasons. Seeing a plant in its natural situation gives knowledge of its needs in cultivation. And then, once design and planting have formed a garden, the process reverses as the garden becomes the inspiration for learning about the natural world.

With the widespread loss of the world's natural habitats now causing the daily extinction of species, botanic gardens and other specialist gardens are becoming as arks, holding irreplaceable collections. Thus gardens are increasingly cooperating to form networks which can retain as great a diversity of plants as possible. More than ever gardens can offer a refuge for our beleaguered flora and fauna and, whether a garden be great or small, formal or natural, this need should underpin its enduring qualities of peace and harmony – the challenge of the creative unison of formal and natural areas.

The authors of these volumes have all become acknowledged specialists in particular aspects of gardening and their texts draw on their experience and impart the vitality that sustains their own enthusiasm and dedication. It is hoped, therefore, that these *Kew Gardening Guides* will be the means of sharing their hard-earned knowledge and understanding with a wider audience.

Like a many faceted gemstone, horticulture has many sides, each with its own devotees, but plants are the common link, and they define this series of horticultural books and the work of Kew itself.

John Simmons
Editor

Introduction

This is a book for enthusiasts about a genus of shrubs of the greatest interest to both amateur and professional gardeners, whether for greenhouse cultivation, for use as summer features in the garden or even, in the case of the hardy cultivars, for permanent garden planting. The fuchsia is enjoying its second great peak of popularity – the first was in the late nineteenth century – and seems likely to remain one of the most popular greenhouse and garden shrubs for many years to come.

The difference between growing fuchsias in the Victorian era and now is that horticultural science has made such great advances in recent years. The wealth of accumulated information available to gardeners has grown accordingly, and there is also a whole range of gadgets and labour-saving aids for the garden and greenhouse, together with effective chemicals to combat pests and diseases. In response to the dramatic rise in the cost of all fuels, industry has responded by producing a range of accurately calibrated propagators and heating equipment. As far as fuchsias are concerned, the range of colours and flower size has been considerably increased since Victorian times.

To enable readers of this book to make the most effective use of modern equipment, vague recommendations and loosely defined terms have been avoided when precise figures can be quoted on fertilizer applications, humidity readings, temperatures, light levels, etc. More technical information than usual has therefore been included in some chapters, though appraisal of the best traditional practices is also given. Once the new concepts have been mastered, they will give a greater insight into the basis of modern horticulture. These recommendations are not necessarily intended to be followed to the letter, but are those commonly used in general commercial practice. They are intended for initial guidance in the hope that the newcomer to growing fuchsias will have a successful first growing season, and that the enthusiast will use them as the basis for further experimentation and continued progress. One of the aims of the book is to bridge the gap between the relative newcomer to gardening and the experienced amateur or professional grower.

Luckily not all the processes involved in growing fuchsias can be closely defined, or much of the pleasure derived from growing them would be lost. No two plants are ever alike, and skilled human intervention is often needed when they fail to make the expected progress under apparently ideal conditions. The training of fuchsias into special shapes, too, is a subtle blend of art and science that will continue to defy the imposition of rigid schedules or blueprint growing.

Well informed professionals and a few amateur growers are propagating many species of plants by the modern process of tissue culture. This new method is ideal for the production of a limited number of cultivars in large quantities, but as the fuchsia is so easy to propagate by traditional methods, tissue culture has not been included in this work.

1
The Fuchsia Story

The first fuchsia was discovered by Father Charles Plumier, a missionary working in Santo Domingo. He published details of this discovery in 1703 and called the new plant *Fuchsia triphylla flore coccinea* after Leonhart Fuchs, who had once occupied the chair of medicine at the University of Tübingen. This original plant is still known today as *Fuchsia triphylla*, and its influence is very noticeable in a popular group of hybrids derived from it.

The first fuchsia to reach England was probably *Fuchsia coccinea*; the event was recorded by Solander in Aiton's *Hortus Kewensis* and *The Botanical Magazine* of 1789. It was at the end of the eighteenth century that other fuchsia species were introduced, such as *F. magellanica* and *F. arborescens*, with *F. fulgens* following in the early nineteenth century. The first crosses between species were made at about this time, and although the results of early hybridizing are not known, it seems likely that these original species were the ancestors of most of our modern fuchsia hybrids.

The fuchsia species known today all come from Central and South America, New Zealand and Tahiti. They range in size from trees such as *F. excorticata* down to low, creeping plants such as *F. procumbens*. Others, such as *F. tunariensis* and *F. tuberosa*, are epiphytic rather than growing directly in the ground, and thrive in the vegetable detritus that collects in the forks of trees or on rocks. It is interesting to note that wherever the species are found, the nature of the site is such that the climatic conditions are always cool and moist. All the modern hybrids have inherited the dislike of a hot, dry atmosphere.

Although the progress of fuchsia hybridization from 1820 onwards is virtually unrecorded, we can assume that steady progress was made until, in late Victorian times, the fuchsia was at its first great peak of popularity. This state continued until the First World War, which imposed completely new priorities on gardeners, and the cultivation of fuchsias declined. At the end of the war there were new fashions in plant popularity. The Victorian period rapidly receded into distant memory and the fuchsia was regarded as a symbol of the past.

Luckily, the best of the hybrids produced up to that time remained in cultivation. In the 1930s a selection of these, and also some from French sources, were taken to the United States. The American growers set to work and created virtually a new race of hybrids, which found their way back to Britain in the 1950s. The large flowers, some with appealing new colours in pastel shades, created instant interest and helped to start a second great wave of popularity, which continues unabated today.

The botanical family Onagraceae is divided into twenty-one separate but related groups of plants. Each of these groups is termed a genus (plural genera), and the group of plants known collectively as *Fuchsia* makes up one of them. A genus is a group whose individual members are clearly related to each other by the possession of certain common characteristics. These individual members, or species, can be distinguished from each other by important but less fundamental

Opposite: *Fuchsia coccinea* as depicted in *The Botanical Magazine*, plate 97, 1789

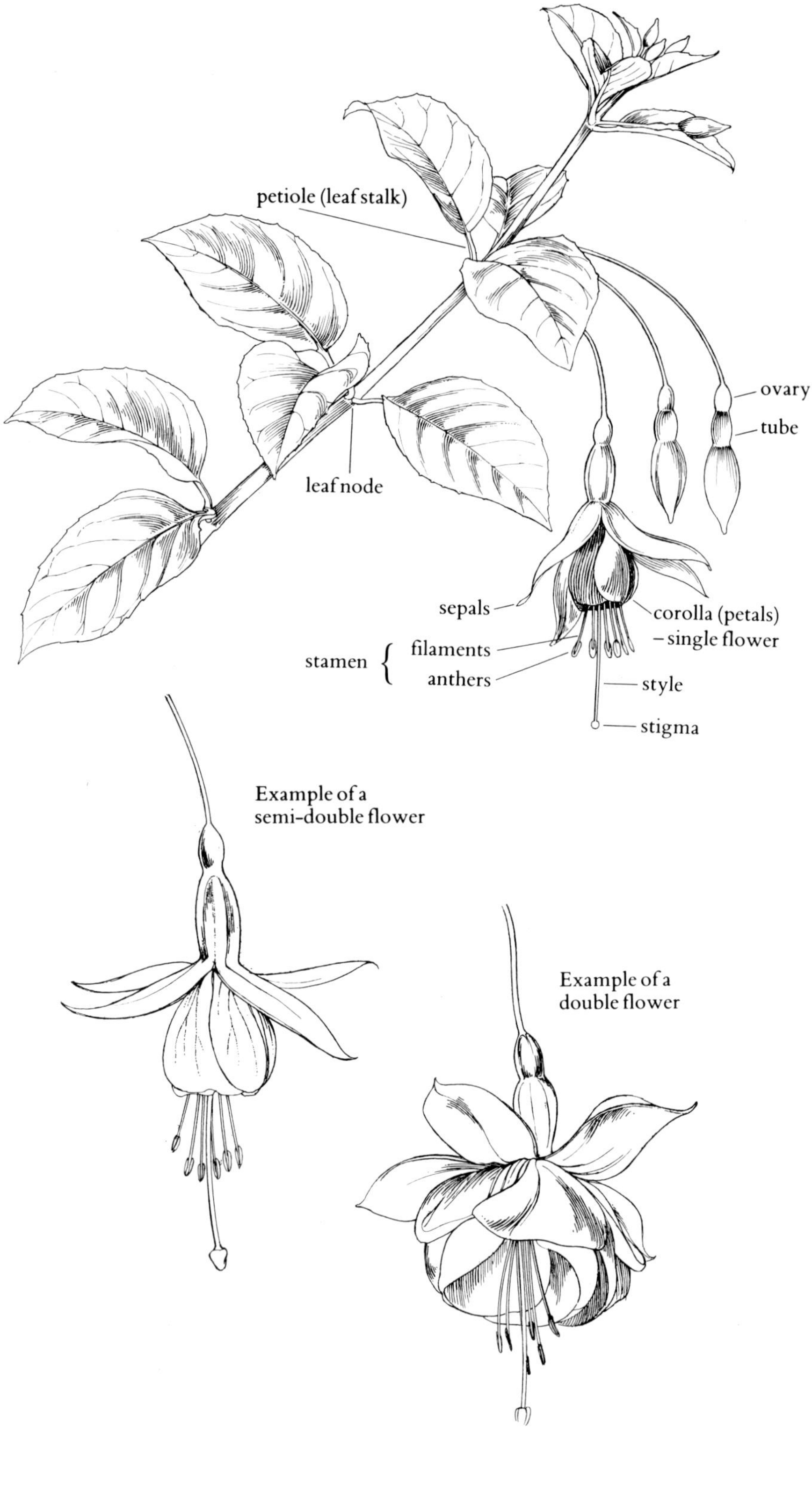

The fuchsia flower.
This illustration explains the nomenclature used to describe the various parts of the fuchsia plant. Fuchsias with a corolla comprising only four petals are described as single flowered, and those with eight petals are termed doubles. Semi-double flowers have five to seven petals, but they are often classified with the doubles for exhibition purposes

differences. When two plants are so similar that they must be regarded as a single species but still have some minor difference, such as flower colour, that can be easily noted, they are called varieties. For example, *F. magellanica* var. *molinae* only differs from *F. magellanica* by having pinkish-white flowers instead of red and purple. These varieties originated without the assistance of man, and have been recorded growing wild in their natural habitat. New plants that have been produced in cultivation either naturally or artificially are called cultivars (cultivated varieties). The terms variety and cultivar are not the same in meaning, and they are used for separate purposes. The majority of fuchsias commercially available today are correctly referred to as cultivars.

The genus *Fuchsia*, which consists of approximately one hundred separate species, can be arranged into related sections within the genus. (A survey of this work will be found in a paper by Dr P.A. Munz entitled 'A Revision of the Genus Fuchsia (Onagraceae)' in the *Proceedings of the California Academy of Sciences* 25, (1), 1–138 (1943).) The other genera within the family Onagraceae contain familiar garden plants such as clarkia, godetia, willow herb and the evening primrose (*Oenothera biennis*).

2
Fuchsias under Glass

The information given in the following sections is based on experience gained at approximately latitude 52° at sea level in Europe. Growers in other areas who experience different climatic conditions or seasons may need to modify their cultural techniques accordingly.

Cultural needs

Light

In most European countries fuchsias will only need to be shaded in the greenhouse during the hottest part of the year. In a large, well ventilated house this need will be minimal and the light level should only be reduced by 10 to 20 per cent, whereas in a small, poorly ventilated house it could be reduced by as much as 30 per cent. This decrease in light level is necessary not because the plants will be harmed by bright light but to keep the temperature and humidity to within tolerable limits.

The degree of shading can be altered by using commercial shade netting or blinds designed to give a known light reduction, or by painting or spraying the outside of the glass with a proprietary shading compound. Any uncertainty in the level of light reduction afforded by these methods can be checked by using a photographic light meter; a 25 per cent reduction in light level is equivalent to a half stop reduction on the meter reading. If a light meter is not available, a friendly photographer might be persuaded to help in exchange for being allowed to photograph the fuchsia collection.

The most efficient means of shading is by blinds or netting placed close to, but not touching, the outside of the greenhouse. White shading material, which is superior to the green version, painted on the outside of the glass is next best, whereas netting placed inside the greenhouse is least efficient. In an average season shading should not be needed at all from the end of September through to the beginning of March.

Composts

A distinction must be made between potting composts and the material made in the garden compost heap; they are completely different products and they are used for separate purposes.

The types of potting compost in current use can be divided into two sorts: those which contain loam or soil as an essential ingredient (i.e. John Innes composts), and those which do not (i.e. soilless composts). The latter mixtures are based on peat, pulverized bark or other inert materials such as perlite, vermiculite, rock wool or sand.

An essential requirement of any potting compost is that it should contain all the mineral salts in proper proportions to supply the needs of the plant and to provide anchorage and moisture for the roots. There must always be, within

Opposite: 'Trumpeter' (see page 113)

certain tolerances, a relationship between the air and water contained in a compost, as the air–water ratio dictates the types of bacteria that grow in it. Unfavourable bacteria will grow if the compost is overwatered or if an unsuitable compost material that excludes air is used, and this will lead to souring of the soil and will cause the roots to rot. The firmness of potting also alters the air–water ratio in the compost, especially with the more spongy, soilless mixtures, and it is therefore very important to follow the manufacturer's recommendations in this respect.

A feature of the John Innes soil based composts is that there is a chemical reaction, caused by the fertilizers, which renders them toxic and unsuitable for use if not used within approximately six weeks after preparation. Some manufacturers extend the shelf life of the product by packing the fertilizer in a separate container which has to be mixed with the rest of the ingredients immediately before use. Once mixed, however, this compost must still be used within the specified period. Soilless composts are also best used fresh, but if they are stored according to the manufacturers' instructions they will last for relatively long periods and can generally be kept from one season to the next.

The mineral salts that are essential for plant growth are normally found in the soil in weak solutions. In any greater concentration these same salts can scorch roots and even kill a plant. An important property of soil is to 'lock up' relatively large quantities of plant nutrients, thus rendering them safe to plant tissue, but making more available at the same rate as the plant roots can assimilate them. This is called a buffering effect; it is not found in peat or any other compost ingredients, and is one of the main differences between soil based and soilless products. John Innes potting compost can contain a large supply of fertilizer without fear of any damage to the plant roots growing in it, and it is therefore

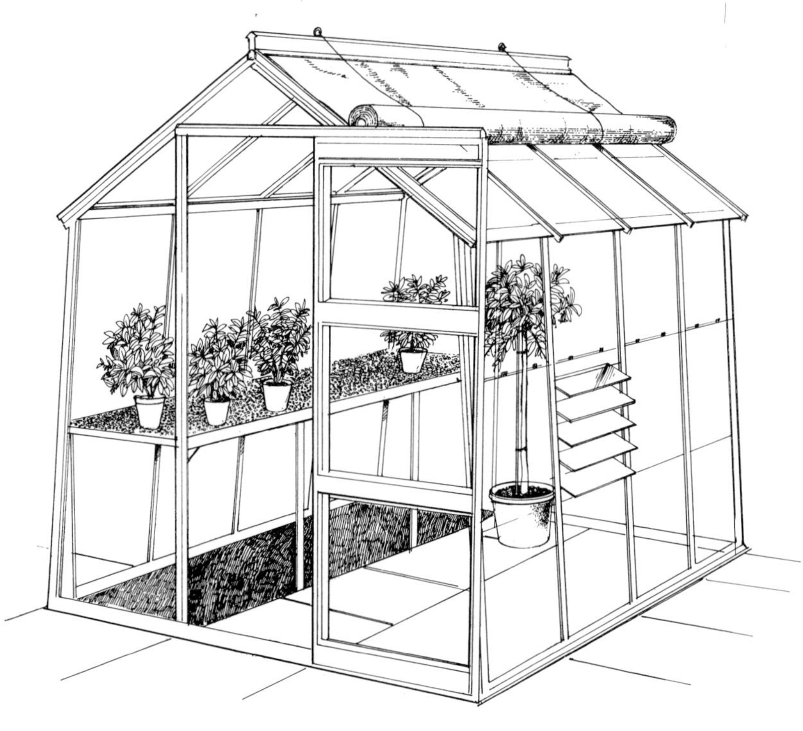

Even a well-ventilated greenhouse will need shading in summer to reduce the internal temperature and to prevent the atmosphere from becoming too dry. Shading can be provided by external roller blinds, by special paints applied to the outside of the glass or by pinning up shade netting inside the structure

unnecessary to start feeding a plant growing in it as soon as one growing in a soilless medium.

Slow release fertilizers have been developed which, as their name implies, are designed to release their nutrient content slowly and reliably over a period of many months, and in general these products work very well in combination with soilless composts. However, whichever type of compost is used, it will eventually become exhausted and it is necessary to supplement it with more fertilizer (see section on feeding on p. 28). When this additional feeding is required the buffering effect of loam or soil makes the process less critical and the danger of overfeeding is much reduced.

With all the stated advantages of soil based composts it would seem inconsistent to use anything else, but in practice suitable loam for the manufacture of John Innes composts is in short supply and is of variable quality, and even under closely controlled conditions different batches of product from the same manufacturer can give very uneven results. On the other hand, soilless composts vary little from batch to batch, and are cheaper to produce as well as more consistent in quality. Most professional growers almost always use soilless composts.

The amateur grower would be well advised to use one of the proprietary soilless composts for propagation and early potting, when little supplementary feeding is required, and to change, if desired, to a soil based compost in pot sizes above 10 cm (4 in). The extra weight of soil based composts can be an advantage as it stabilizes large or tall specimens, such as standard trained fuchsias, and it provides more anchorage for the base of the supporting cane or stake.

The roots of most young plants, including fuchsias, which are growing in a peat based compost are often reluctant to move from it into a soil based medium. It is better to make an intermediate potting into a small container using a peat based compost which contains a good proportion of grit or other drainage material (one part by volume to four parts by volume of compost) and then, when the roots are well established in this medium, potting on into a soil based mixture.

The choice between the John Innes and the soilless composts is largely a personal matter as the highest possible results are obtainable in either medium provided that appropriate modifications in technique are made in accordance with their different properties. In general, most growers will opt for John Innes No. 2 (or No. 3 in the case of very large specimens), or any of the commercially available soilless composts except those formulated for growing specialized subjects such as ericas or cacti.

No additives or modifications should be necessary for any of the commercial composts, except perhaps for the addition of some coarse grit or perlite (about 10 to 15 per cent by volume) to those peat based composts which do not already contain them. The acidity of the standard commercial potting composts will be found to be entirely suitable for fuchsias.

Pots and potting

Plastic pots have been obtainable now for several decades and at the time of their introduction there was much discussion, often heated, as to their superiority or otherwise over the traditional clay pot. These discussions are still going on today.

Opposite: 'Golden Marinka', a cultivar with variegated foliage (see page 96)

The main difference between these two types of pot, apart from their weight and appearance, is the difference in porosity of the materials from which they are made. Clay pots are very porous, and help to reduce the effects of overwatering at the critical early stages but tend to dry out too rapidly when the plant is large and well established. However, the porosity of the clay pot in conjunction with the evaporating water film over its surface keeps the soil in this type of container measurably cooler than in other types of pot, especially the black plastic ones. This temperature difference is important to fuchsias, which as a group dislike high temperatures, but by standing a plastic pot inside another larger one this difference between the two types can largely be eliminated.

Most modern composts have been formulated for use with plastic pots and as they are, at the present time, much easier to obtain than clay ones and are more pleasant and clean to use, they are the obvious choice for the majority of gardeners.

Potting up plants is really a matter of common sense, but rooted cuttings must be held by their leaves and not by their stems. A bruised or torn leaf will seldom kill a plant, but a bruised or broken stem could spell disaster. The technique of potting is always the same whatever size of plant is being handled. The aim is to get the new compost into intimate contact with the roots by light pressure with the fingers, or preferably by tapping or slapping the side of the pot as the compost is being introduced. The moisture content of the compost at the time of potting is not critical but it should not be used in a very dry condition. The use of wet compost is not harmful but it is sticky and unpleasant to use.

Right: Fuchsias grow best in cool or moderately warm conditions. In hot weather the root system can become overheated when the pots are in direct light; this is very likely to happen when the plants are growing in black plastic pots. It can be overcome by standing the pot inside another, larger pot so that the air gap insulates the root system. Because of water evaporation from the surface, clay pots keep the soil ball cooler than plastic pots and do not need this treatment

The newly potted plant should be at the same depth or slightly deeper than it was originally, and there should be enough space left between the top of the pot and the surface of the soil so that sufficient water can be given in one application

to soak the entire contents of the pot. This feature is especially important with large plants in hot weather.

Young, well rooted cuttings are normally planted up in early spring into 9 cm ($3\frac{1}{2}$ in) pots using a soilless compost, and under correct conditions their progress will be rapid and the plants will then need to be repotted at regular intervals. An advantage of plastic pots is that the root ball can be easily slid out of them without damage for the roots to be inspected. As soon as the roots can be seen throughout the compost the plant is ready for potting on into a 10–13 cm (4–5 in) container.

Well-rooted cuttings should be potted up before growth is checked. Handle the young plant carefully as a bruised stem can seriously damage the plant

Well-rooted young plants will need to be potted on into larger containers at regular intervals. Small plants in 6.5 to 8 cm ($2\frac{1}{2}$ to 3 in) pots can be moved into 9 to 11.5 cm ($3\frac{1}{2}$ to $4\frac{1}{2}$ in) pots, and larger plants in 9 to 13 cm ($3\frac{1}{2}$ to 5 in) pots can be moved into 13 to 18 cm (5 to 7 in) pots respectively. Water sparingly for at least two weeks or until the plants are seen to be doing well

By mid-summer the plants should be in full flower and a further move, into 18 cm (7 in) pots, will help to reduce the need for frequent watering and to sustain growth, which will in turn encourage the production of more flower buds. Certain vigorous cultivars and most second-year plants will eventually need even larger pots, but if John Innes composts have been used the root action of the plants will be less vigorous and somewhat smaller pots will suffice.

Watering

After the purchase of a new plant at a nursery the customer often asks for advice on the frequency of watering. A truthful but somewhat unhelpful answer in this case would be 'whenever it needs it'. There is no single easy answer, and in nursery practice the decision about when to water and feed the plants is usually taken by one of the most experienced staff working there. An assumption is made that the reader of this book will either be watering the plants by hand or will be using some system of semi-automatic irrigation such as capillary matting, rather than the more complex, often fully automated systems used by commercial growers.

A plant which has just been repotted or potted for the first time should be watered immediately, but only just enough should be given to settle the plant into its pot and to bring the roots into intimate contact with the new compost. Thorough soaking of the compost at this time must be avoided or the soil will quickly become sour. Fuchsias are particularly sensitive to overwatering in the early stages of growth, and the need for care at this critical time cannot be overemphasized. Most of the water contained in the compost is drained out by the roots growing in it, and only a small proportion evaporates from the soil surface. Until the roots of a newly potted plant thoroughly penetrate all the compost there is always a danger of causing damage to the roots by overwatering. If, after the initial watering, hot weather causes the surface of the soil around a newly potted plant to dry out, only enough water should be given to dampen the surface layers, for the compost under the surface will in all probability still be adequately moist. However, as soon as the roots fully permeate the compost it is vital that sufficient water is applied to wet thoroughly the complete soil ball. Once the surface layer of soil around an established plant appears dry, the lower layers are probably also dry and the plant will need watering.

In hot summer weather fuchsias need a lot of moisture and the plants should not be allowed to wilt for the lack of it. This will probably mean daily watering; the need to water more frequently than this is an indication that it is time to move the plant into a larger pot. In hot weather the plants can be watered whenever the condition of the soil indicates that it is needed, but watering must be gradually reduced and maintained at a lower level during the winter months. (This aspect is dealt with under overwintering on p. 32.)

During early spring, when it is difficult to ventilate the greenhouse, it is of value to keep the plants slightly drier than usual to help to discourage the formation of over-soft growth.

The dryness of the soil can be assessed by touch or by learning to gauge the moisture content of the compost by its colour. All composts are darker in colour when wet and gradually become paler when they dry out. This colour change is most noticeable with soilless composts, and most experienced commercial growers, with due allowance for the state of maturity of the crop, can tell at a glance by the appearance of the soil surface whether it needs watering.

The actual moment when watering is required is very difficult to describe. The surface of the soil in the pot will be decidedly dry but not at the point where the plant starts to wilt because of lack of moisture. Little harm will be done, however, if on occasions the plants are accidentally allowed to become too dry, and this is preferable to continual overwatering. Another useful tip is to compare the weight of the potted plant when the soil is dry and after watering. The weight difference is very marked, and when sufficient experience has been gained this technique can be a useful further guide to the need for water.

Experience is the only real guide to when water is required, but once this

'Cotton Candy' (see page 92)

'Tennessee Waltz'
(see page 112)

knowledge is gained the newcomer to pot plant gardening is well on the way to becoming a proficient grower, as one of the most difficult aspects of this type of gardening will have been mastered. Some of the early formulations of soilless composts were difficult to rewet if inadvertently allowed to become too dry. This problem has largely been overcome by the addition of wetting agents, and most brands of this sort of compost are now just as easy to rewet as the soil based types.

It does not matter whether water is applied to the surface of the soil or allowed to soak up from the bottom of the pot. The aim, at least with an established plant, is to wet the whole soil ball, and the result should be the same using either method. If the need for watering is assessed by the colour of the soil surface, an allowance must be made if the plants are watered from below by standing them on capillary matting, or by other similar methods, as often the lower layers of soil are wetter than the appearance of the surface suggests.

The quality of water used for irrigation is not critical, and most normal sources that are considered suitable for horticultural purposes can be used, but rainwater must be stored in clean containers and kept in complete darkness. Some mains water supplies in hard-water areas will eventually give rise to nutritional problems because of an excessive build-up of salts in the soil; to correct the problem the plants should be repotted more often than is usually necessary.

Feeding

Once any plant has become well established in a pot it will already have absorbed most of the nutrients originally contained in the potting compost; if subsequent growth is not to suffer the plant will need either to be re-potted or to be given supplementary feeding. In early stages of growth, when the plant is small, the aim in general is to pot on the subject into fresh compost as soon as the soil ball is well filled with roots. If for some reason this action cannot be taken at the appropriate time, an occasional liquid feed should be applied to prevent a check to growth. When the plant is well established in its final pot regular feeding will be needed.

Fertilizer can be added in a number of ways; there are now various tablets and spikes which can be placed in the soil, powders to sprinkle on the surface of the soil and even fertilizer mats to place under the plant pot. All these products work, and the specific instructions supplied by each manufacturer should be followed very carefully. However, the most popular – and arguably the best – means of supplementary feeding is by supplying diluted liquid feed as part of the general watering procedure. This method has the advantage that the knowledgeable gardener can, as circumstances and growing conditions change, alter the formulation of the feed used. Such flexibility is impossible with most of the other methods of supplementary feeding.

The point at which feeding should start depends on the rate of growth of the plant and the type of potting compost which has been used. Generally, after potting up or re-potting a plant into fresh compost, no feeding will be required for the first four to six weeks, but for plants growing in a soil based compost this period should be increased to eight to twelve weeks. The progress of the plant, the vigour of the particular cultivar used and the prevailing temperature and light levels also need to be considered.

At first, as the potting compost still contains a reserve of nutrients, only occasional feeding will be needed, but as the plant progresses and the roots ramify throughout the soil mass, the plant is entirely dependent on the grower to supply its complete needs and the frequency of feeding will have to be increased. The instructions supplied with proprietary liquid feeds generally assume that the latter condition applies, so the feed should be supplied to younger plants less frequently or in a more diluted form. An allowance must also be made for the season and state of growth: a plant growing rapidly in summer will need more frequent feeding than a near dormant plant in winter.

Fuchsias are quite greedy, and large plants in active growth or flower will require weekly or even twice weekly feeds, while monthly feeds are sufficient for plants which are growing only slowly in winter. It is always better to give frequent weak feeds rather than infrequent heavy doses, and it is quite acceptable to use the manufacturer's weekly recommended dose in two half strength, twice weekly feeds.

It is also important to understand that there is a link between the frequency of watering and the frequency of feeding. If a plant needs water two or three times a week it will not need feeding more than once every seven to ten days, but if daily watering is required it will probably need feeding every four to five days.

All these factors are a matter of experienced judgement, and it is important to anticipate the need for supplementary feeding; once the plant starts to show symptoms of starvation the problems are very difficult to correct, though subsequent growth, formed after feeding has commenced, will be perfectly normal.

The major elements required for plant growth are nitrogen, phosphorus and potassium, but other elements, including magnesium, calcium, iron, boron, manganese, molybdenum, zinc and copper, which are required in small quantities, are equally vital for healthy growth. Nitrogen and potassium (potash) are the only two elements whose levels, relative to each other, are commonly adjusted for optimum growth. All the other elements should be available in just sufficient quantities to satisfy the needs of the plant, and this detail is taken care of by the dilution instructions given by the fertilizer manufacturer.

Nitrogen and potassium have approximately opposite effects on plant growth. An excess of potassium over nitrogen leads to smaller leaves, a harder, woody appearance to the plant and the production of many, well coloured flowers. An excess of nitrogen over potassium produces large, dark green leaves on a softer, fast growing plant, but at the expense of flowers.

The climatic conditions in winter tend to produce soft growth, and because in summer harder, more sturdy growth is formed, it is customary to vary the nitrogen–potassium balance of the fertilizer to counteract these effects and achieve optimum growth throughout the year.

The analysis or percentage composition of all fertilizers is now stated on the container, and it is necessary to examine the small print to ensure that the correct composition is being selected. Because the relative balance between the nutrients is most important, rather than their absolute concentration, it is customary to refer to the composition of a fertilizer in terms of a ratio between the three major elements. Hence a 1:1:1 fertilizer would contain equal amounts of nitrogen (N), phosphorus (P) and potassium (K), always expressed in that order. For reasons that are only of interest to chemists, the percentage composition of each major element is expressed as nitrogen (total nitrogen, N), phosphorus as phosphorus pentoxide ((P_2O_5) and potassium as potassium oxide (K_2O). Two fertilizers of, for example, percentage composition 10 per cent N, 10 per cent P_2O_5, 10 per cent K_2O (10:10:10 NPK), and 22 per cent N, 22 per cent P_2O_5, 22 per cent K_2O (22:22:22 NPK), are both in effect 1:1:1 NPK fertilizers and can, subject to the manufacturers' recommended dilutions, be used for the same purpose. A 1:1:1 NPK fertilizer is regarded as a normal balance; those of a 2:1:1 or 3:1:1 formulation are high nitrogen fertilizers, and 1:1:2 or 1:1:3 formulations correspondingly high in potassium. It is not important to find a fertilizer to an exact formula; for example, one of the most popular plant foods available has a stated composition of 10:10:27 NPK. This ratio is near enough 1:1:3 NPK, so it can be used whenever a high potassium feed is beneficial.

The phosphorus (phosphate) content of most potting composts is generally adequate for a long period of growth, but the addition of further supplies in the supplementary feed will do no harm in most circumstances. However, in areas of very hard water phosphates react with calcium contained in the water supply to form insoluble calcium phosphates, which in sufficient concentration will collect on the surface of the soil and form a hard, unsightly crust around the rim of the pot, and also impair growth. The cure is to re-pot the plant into fresh compost or to prevent the problem occurring by the occasional use of a feed without added phosphates, such as a 2:0:1, 1:0:1, or 1:0:2 NPK formulation. At least one manufacturer markets these products for both the amateur and the professional grower.

In general, use a feed with a high potassium content during autumn, winter and spring but change to a 1:1:1 or a higher nitrogen feed in summer when the plants are in full flower. During the flowering period the fuchsias' rate of stem growth is greatly reduced, for much of the energy is going into the production of flowers, so unless growth is somewhat stimulated at this stage by providing extra nitrogen, the flowering season may be curtailed or the plant may only produce an irregular succession of blooms.

Overfeeding must be avoided, as an excess of the nitrogen-containing components of the fertilizer will gradually kill the roots, causing the plant to droop in hot weather and then eventually collapse and die. (See also the section on physiological disorders on p. 72.)

If these instructions seem complicated it is as well to remember that a little plant food, whatever its composition, will in most circumstances provide benefit to the plants, and is better than allowing them to deteriorate through starvation. Controlling the quality of growth of the plants by varying the composition of the feed can have a noticeable effect and is worthwhile for the serious grower, but it is not dramatic – and not absolutely necessary for producing acceptably good plants. One of the characteristics of fuchsias is that they are extremely unfussy in their requirements, which is one reason for their popularity.

Opposite:
'Hampshire Blue'
(see page 96)

Right:
'Peppermint Stick'
(see page 105)

Temperature and humidity

The fuchsia is a very tolerant plant, and some of the species and cultivars are hardy enough to be cultivated permanently out of doors in some regions; the majority, although correctly regarded as non-hardy, are in most cases only marginally so. For most cultivars under the protection of a greenhouse or similar structure, therefore, only minimal artificial heating is required. In practice a minimum winter temperature of 5–7°C (40–50°F) is quite adequate for the majority of cultivars, though 10°C (50°F) is needed for some of the species and for hybrids derived from *Fuchsia triphylla*.

The maximum temperature that the plants will receive in the summer is largely dictated by the weather and by the design of the structure in which they are housed. The type of heating apparatus employed is not important provided that it is properly installed and is recognized as being suitable for horticultural purposes.

The humidity of the air surrounding the plants is inextricably linked to the temperature. As the temperature rises the atmosphere will become drier – to the detriment of the fuchsias – unless there is water available to evaporate into the air. When the temperatures are regularly rising to 21–27°C (70–80°F) the floor and pathways within the greenhouse must be regularly dampened to provide a humid atmosphere. Failure to take this precaution when temperatures regularly rise up to or above this higher limit can, with some cultivars, cause leaf and bud fall. Under such conditions the plants are better out of doors; many amateur growers will as a matter of course transfer their plants into the open during the summer.

It is also of great benefit to the plants to mist over the foliage early each morning or evening with a fine-water spray. The water should preferably be clean rainwater, as hard mains water will often leave unsightly marks on the foliage. This regular spraying should be adopted as a standard technique throughout the spring and summer months as it is of great value to the plants, and is a widely accepted means of improving their quality when they are growing under glass. Spraying must be discontinued when the plants are in full bloom, as it sometimes produces disfiguring marks on the flowers. Plants grown in the open will receive the benefit of night-time dew and will thrive accordingly, and the invigorating nature of the open air generally prevents the 'damping off' or damage to the flowers.

OVERWINTERING

The method chosen for overwintering the plants will usually depend on the facilities available. The ideal conditions are those offered by a heated greenhouse or conservatory, but winter storage of specimen plants is still possible without using any heat at all.

Mature plants from previous seasons or plants that were propagated early in the current season can be overwintered by any of the methods described below. Younger plants – those rooted in late summer or autumn – will be unlikely to survive except under warm conditions. If a warm greenhouse or conservatory is not available, young plants are best kept indoors on a moderately warm and bright windowsill.

Some writers suggest that for the continued vigour of fuchsia plants it is essential to rest them in winter by withholding water and forcing them to become dormant. This statement is gradually becoming recognized as being untrue. Plants that live in warm, frost-free countries grow continuously throughout the year, and continue to thrive for many decades. Dormancy needs to be induced only when plants are to be subjected to low temperatures or if a saving in fuel cost is required.

The following section is divided into three parts, according to various different minimum winter temperatures.

Overwintering in a greenhouse heated to 5–13°C (40–55°F)

These are probably the ideal winter conditions for housing a fuchsia collection, and very few losses should be expected. The upper limit of the temperatures quoted will be necessary for any specially tender cultivars such as the *F. triphylla* hybrids and any other particularly tender sorts. An advantage of this method of overwintering is that the plants will continue to make growth, albeit slowly, throughout the colder months of the year. This can be an important point when

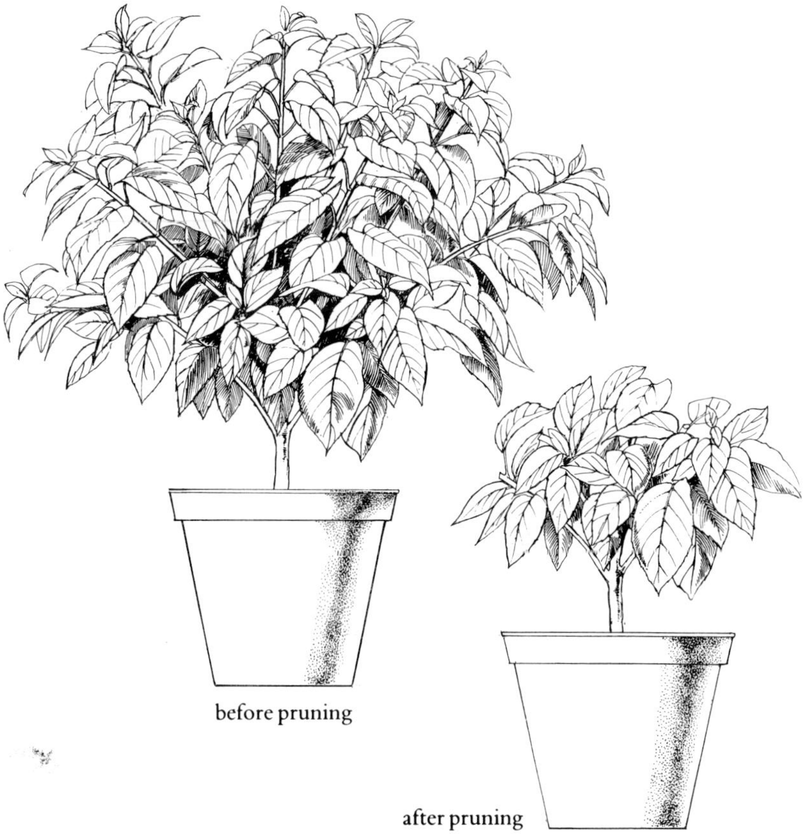

Pruning pot-grown plants. Before the onset of winter, about half of each stem should be pruned away to leave a well-shaped framework for the production of new growth in the following season. Do not prune hardy fuchsias in the garden until growth starts in the spring

very large specimen plants or standard trained fuchsias are being grown.

In September or October established plants that have been grown in pots under glass should be pruned back by cutting off approximately half of each main branch, in such a way that the plant not only retains the original shape in which it was trained but if possible improves upon it. Pruning should always be done with sharp instruments to avoid crushing or bruising the ends of the stems.

Watering must continue throughout the winter period but overwatering must be avoided at all costs. It is very much better gradually to harden the plants by reducing their water supply to the minimum possible, without actually causing them undue distress.

Fuchsias that have been grown outside in beds or containers should be lifted before their growth is checked by cold weather, and up to two thirds of each stem trimmed back as described above. Do not be afraid to prune back hard at this time, when the roots have been disturbed, as it helps to maintain the natural balance between the root system and the aerial portions of the plant. Most of the old soil can be removed from the roots by carefully shaking them, and the plants are then re-potted in fresh compost, using the smallest size of pot that will comfortably accommodate the root system.

Great care will be needed with subsequent watering until the plants are re-established. Any decaying parts of leaves, flowers or fruit should also be removed, and it is a good idea to spray the plants thoroughly with a fungicide containing benomyl or iprodione to control grey mould. Because conditions are still suitable for growth, flowering may recommence, but it will generally cease at about the turn of the year. In the spring, if a minimum night temperature of 13°C (55°F) is maintained many cultivars will start flowering again in May.

Opposite: 'Nellie Nuttall' (see page 104)

Right: 'Hampshire Treasure' (see page 96)

Overwintering in a greenhouse heated to 0–5°C (32–40°F)

Photosynthesis is the process by which a plant manufactures complex plant foods by taking the energy received from sunlight, carbon dioxide from the air and the mineral salts obtained from the soil. This process ceases below an average temperature of about 10°C (50°F). During the coldest months of the year when the average temperature is low the plants will stop growing.

Plants which are already in pots should be trimmed back as described in the previous section, but as the temperature continues to fall watering should be gradually reduced until, in the coldest months of the year, it is withheld altogether. Although the soil surrounding the roots must be on the dry side to prevent rotting, it is essential that it does not dry out completely or the plants will die. Some writers have suggested that as many fuchsia plants die in winter as a result of dryness at the roots as do those killed by frost.

If this method of overwintering is to be a success it is vital that the minimum temperatures does not fall below freezing point, and it is probably better to set the heaters to a degree or two above this level to allow for a suitable margin of error. The heating system must also have sufficient capacity to ensure that this vital minimum temperature is maintained, even on the coldest nights. The use of a maximum–minimum thermometer is essential to confirm this. Many heating systems appear to work perfectly satisfactorily when inspected during the day, but without recourse to such a recording instrument it is only possible to guess what the temperature falls to during the night. The acquisition of a maximum–minimum thermometer, and the subsequent discovery of unacceptably low minimum temperatures, has solved many problems associated with the loss of a large number of plants in winter.

As warmer weather approaches and the average temperature within the greenhouse begins to rise, the plants will start to grow again. The timing of this will vary from area to area and from year to year, but some time in March the plants should generally be showing signs of growth, and watering can then be increased. This is also a good time to trim the stems lightly and to re-pot the overwintered plants. With normal progress, flowering – starting with the single flowered cultivars – will begin some time in June.

Overwintering in the unheated greenhouse

This method, which involves no heating, can be quite attractive in these days of high fuel costs, and it is certainly better than trying to overwinter tender sorts in the open or unprotected in a poorly lit garage or shed. (See also the section on overwintering in the garden on p. 41.)

Unlike plants that are to be kept growing during the winter, they should be left for as long as possible in the open, or in the cold greenhouse, to harden up the stems and to induce dormancy. If the plants out of doors are subjected to a slight frost so much the better.

Before very severe weather is expected the plants must be lifted from the open or taken from their containers, and the soil shaken from the roots. The stems must be trimmed back by at least half, taking care to remove all soft, unripe or damaged wood, leaves, flowers and fruit. The plants are loosely bundled together, laid on their side and completely buried to a depth of 15 cm (6 in) in the greenhouse borders, or they may be laid on the soil and a similar depth of dry peat placed on top of them. It is important that the greenhouse soil or the peat is not dust dry, nor must it be noticeably damp; if the lower layers appear to become dry with the passage of time do not be afraid lightly to water over the surface of the soil. The plants may also be buried in a large box or container within the greenhouse, but if they are kept on the staging they will not be as well insulated as those buried in the soil and will be more likely to freeze. The aim is to provide sufficient insulation around the plants to prevent access by frost and to prevent the plant tissues drying out. Large plants such as standard trained fuchsias can also be stored by this method, as long as the physical size of the plants is not too much of a problem. The availability of a cold greenhouse to protect the plants from late spring frosts is a distinct advantage, and larger plants with earlier flowers can be produced by this means.

When the weather is suitably improved in spring the plants can be moved from their winter quarters and potted up individually in the usual manner. Any dead or unhealthy growth should be pruned away at this stage. If the weather temporarily deteriorates the plants can be protected by placing sheets of newspaper over them on critical nights.

A large, well insulated cold frame can also serve in place of an unheated greenhouse. With average progress flowering can be expected by about mid to late June, which is probably a month earlier than the hardy cultivars that have spent the whole winter in the garden.

Growing for exhibition

The way to grow medal-winning plants is to attend meticulously to all the cultural details. The information in this book will provide a good basis on which to start growing fuchsias for exhibition but with experience it should be possible to experiment and develop original techniques. The secret of success is to understand what fuchsias need, and to meet these needs. This knowledge is gained both by reading to learn the theory of the subject, and then by putting the information into practice.

The principles of growing fuchsias for exhibition are the same as those for producing plants for general decoration, but there are a number of differences that need to be taken into account. There is always a show schedule to be observed. This will give details of any limit to pot sizes, the number of plants allowed in a hanging basket, those cultivars which are acceptable as hardy, etc. The rules must be understood and obeyed or the exhibit may be ruled NAS (Not According to Schedule) and disqualified.

Not all cultivars are equally suited to exhibition. Most experienced showmen will have favourite hybrids, whose every special requirement has been carefully studied so that they can be grown to the peak of perfection. New and potentially promising cultivars will also be grown each year to compare with the standard varieties. The beginner is advised to visit as many of the fuchsia shows as possible, to take notes of those cultivars that have won the prizes, and to make a selection from these as the basis for the show collection. A list of hybrids that have featured widely among the prizewinners is given at the end of this book.

The exhibition fuchsia should be grown to be at its peak on the day of the show, and this requirement means that any special pruning and shaping must

'Leonora' (see page 100)

cease by a certain date to allow the plant to flower and mature in time for the show. As a general guide, for single flowered cultivars this pruning and shaping should stop approximately eight to ten weeks before the required date, and ten to fourteen weeks beforehand for double flowered cultivars.

It is a good idea to prevent premature flowering by picking off unwanted flower buds as soon as they are big enough to handle. This is quite a chore, but the time spent by the grower will be amply repaid by better growth and, when the plant is allowed to mature, a greater abundance of flowers.

Most flower shows are held in the summer, and feeding procedures can be modified to suit these special circumstances. The exhibitor will probably use a high nitrogen fertilizer as often as thought advisable to encourage maximum growth and to make the plant as large as possible. However, three to four weeks before the show, when the plant is in advanced bud, a change to a high potassium feed should be made to improve the flower colour and generally to harden the plant, so that it can be moved to the exhibition hall without undue risk of deterioration or damage.

Most show plants will have been grown by the biennial method described under summer propagation on p. 59. This system has the advantage that it gives enough time to form a good, shapely plant of sufficient size to impress the judges.

Fuchsias as house plants

The fuchsia was a popular Victorian house plant and it also thrived in their temperate conservatories. In the modern centrally heated home conditions are quite different, and the atmosphere is generally too dry to suit the fuchsia. A plant that has been grown in the humid conditions of a greenhouse will very often react quite dramatically when moved into the home. Within a period of twelve hours the open flowers and flower buds can completely fall, followed a little later by the leaves, though the plant will nearly always recover if it is quickly returned to a more suitable climate. Not all fuchsias behave in this way, and some houses seem more favourable to their cultivation than others. Many types of fuchsia can be used as temporary house plants, being returned to the garden or greenhouse when their appearance begins to deteriorate. Tough cultivars, which will usually survive in the most difficult conditions, are 'Display', 'Brutus' and 'Dollar Princess'.

Before moving a plant from the greenhouse it is a good plan to harden it up by keeping it rather on the dry side for a few weeks and then, after the move has been made, to mist spray it occasionally with clean water. All the other processes of feeding, potting and watering are, in general, little different from those described for cultivation in the greenhouse, and all the observations made in that section apply equally here.

Plants from the garden can also be brought indoors for the winter. The best position is a light but cool room so that growth will not be encouraged. The preparation and pruning of the plants before being brought into the house is similar to that described in the section on overwintering.

Fuchsias are ideal plants for growing in a conservatory

M.S. del. J.N. Fitch, lith.

Vincent Brooks, Day & Son, Imp.

3
Fuchsias in the Garden

Permanent planting

The fuchsia is often regarded as a tender plant but there are many cultivars, and some species and their varieties, that will thrive when planted in a permanent position in the garden. Not all districts are suitable, as fuchsias will not survive in areas that experience prolonged or severe frost. The most favourable areas will have a warm summer with regular rainfall or some form of artificial irrigation and a mild, generally frost free winter. In the less favourable areas much can be done to ensure success by choosing a suitably sheltered planting position. It is also essential to choose cultivars that have already proved their worth in outdoor situations. A list of such plants is included at the end of the book.

The soil type available is not important as fuchsias will happily tolerate a wide variety of conditions. Most reasonably fertile garden soils will prove to be suitable, with the exception of those which become waterlogged in winter. A slightly acid soil (pH 6 to 7) is preferred, but the plants will grow well even where there is a chalky subsoil. The main problems here will be caused not by alkalinity but rather by the soil drying out rapidly in summer. Under these conditions it is necessary to water the plants frequently, and to mulch the borders around them to conserve moisture. Existing flower beds will not need any special preparation before fuchsias are planted, but new sites will benefit from the usual cultivation and the addition of well rotted manure or garden compost.

Fuchsias will grow and flower well in full sunshine and partial shade, but those intended for permanent planting in areas where there is a risk of frost are best kept in a sunny position. This will ensure that the stems ripen well in autumn and they will then be in a suitable condition to survive a severe winter.

The best time to plant a hardy fuchsia is in the late spring or early summer after all danger of frost is past. The plant can then become well established before the critical first winter. In particularly bad weather, a hardy fuchsia can be killed back to soil level, and if the base of the stem is near the surface due to shallow planting, it may die completely. The secret of success is to plant the fuchsia with several inches of the stem below soil level and thus protected from frost, so that new growth can if necessary be made from there. However, when a fuchsia is planted in this way precautions must be taken to avoid a severe check to growth. A round depression is made, about 45 cm (18 in) across and 10 cm (4 in) deep. The fuchsia is planted in the centre of this depression in the usual way, with the original soil level about 10 cm (4 in) below that of the rest of the border. The depression is then gradually filled in during the growing season to allow the plant to become accustomed to the change in level. The routine processes of weeding and watering will generally perform this operation automatically without the need for special effort. However, before the start of the first winter the depression must already have been levelled and a certain amount of bracken, leafmould, straw or coarse peat spread over and around the crown of the plant.

Opposite: *Fuchsia triphylla* has a very distinctive flower which is the main characteristic of the group of hybrids derived from this species

In dry weather always water newly planted fuchsias well to ensure rapid establishment and full growth. It is always better to plant out a specimen from a 10 cm (4 in) pot or larger as small plants will not establish themselves so quickly and will consequently be more liable to fail. Smaller plants can be grown on in pots in the greenhouse for up to a year and then hardened off before planting outdoors at the appropriate time.

In autumn, hardy fuchsias should only be very lightly pruned, if at all; when they start to grow in spring the stems are trimmed back to the nearest live bud. Generally the new growth will start to appear in May, and in mild districts fuchsias will start to flower from the end of June onwards, and be at their best throughout the summer and autumn.

Plants such as 'Margaret', *F. magellanica* and the cultivar 'Riccartonii' will make quite large plants in the shrub border, while small – growing plants such as *F. pumila* or 'Tom Thumb' and its sports are suitable for rockeries.

Opposite: Standard fuchsias used in a border. This colourful planting is reminiscent of the bedding schemes so popular during the latter part of the 19th century

Right: Fuchsias make a splendid display in summer when they are planted in borders and in hanging baskets

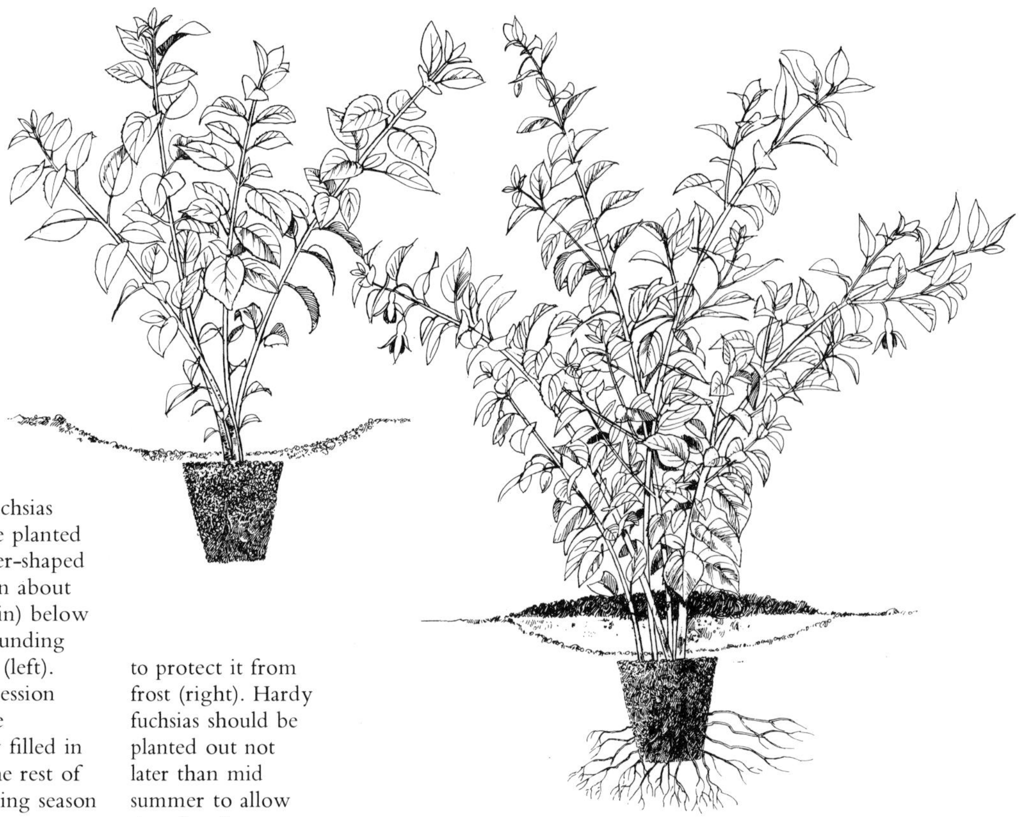

Hardy fuchsias should be planted in a saucer-shaped depression about 10 cm (4 in) below the surrounding soil level (left). The depression should be gradually filled in during the rest of the growing season and coarse peat or bracken placed over the crown of the plant to plant to protect it from frost (right). Hardy fuchsias should be planted out not later than mid summer to allow time for them to become established before the first winter

FUCHSIAS AS HEDGES

A hedge can be used to divide up a garden or as a windbreak to protect tender species in winter. A fuchsia hedge can only be used for the former purpose, as except in favourable districts it will need a little protection itself. However, there are few other subjects that will flower almost continuously throughout the summer and autumn, so a fuchsia hedge is still a good choice for many positions in the garden.

Hedges are usually intended to last for some years, so a little extra care should be taken before planting to ensure that the site is well dug and manured. All the precautions described above in general garden planting should be taken, but the plants for the hedge are conveniently planted in a shallow trench rather than in individual saucer-shaped depressions. The spacing between each plant should be about 45 cm (18 in), though this can be reduced if only a low hedge consisting of dwarf cultivars is required. The pruning of the hedge should normally be restricted to the removal of dead wood when fresh growth starts in the spring. If the hedge grows well, a late summer clipping may also be required, though this can be a difficult decision as the plant will be in full flower.

The appearance of the hedge will be neater if only one cultivar is used for the entire length, as different sorts will inevitably grow at different rates, giving an untidy and unbalanced effect. A list of suitable cultivars for growing as hedges is given at the end of this book.

Fuchsias as temporary garden plants

Although in cold areas the more tender fuchsias cannot be a permanent part of any garden display, they are an invaluable asset in summer planting schemes. The large, pastel-coloured flowers that cascade from many of the modern hybrids are a miracle of plant breeding, and they are difficult to overlook for a long-lasting, spectacular display which will last throughout summer and autumn. Fuchsias are ideal for hanging pots or baskets, window boxes and decorative urns, and as the evening light fades those plants with pale flowers stand out clearly, and greatly enhance the appearance of any patio or loggia.

The preparation and planting of hanging baskets under glass is described in the next chapter. If these baskets are intended for exterior decoration, they should be hung outside on warm days to harden them off, and then returned to the greenhouse at night. After a week of this treatment, and if the danger of night frost is past, they can be left outside permanently for the rest of the season. To lessen the shock before being transferred from the warm, sheltered greenhouse to the relatively severe conditions of the open garden, a similar period of hardening off or gradual acclimatization should be given to any type of fuchsia or other garden plant. In late May or early June bush plants grown from cuttings rooted in the previous summer and housed in a heated greenhouse throughout the winter will probably be in 15 cm (6 in) pots. These plants, which should be in flower or advanced bud, are of tremendous value in the garden. They will fill temporary bare spots in a shrub border or any place that needs the brightening effect of a flowering plant.

A specimen fuchsia looks very effective planted in a decorative urn or small window box, either on its own or in combination with other bedding plants such as petunias or trailing lobelia. Standard and half standard fuchsias can be stood outside in large pots, or they can be planted directly in the soil of an open border. The heads of these plants must be well supported, tied to a very substantial stake and given a sheltered position, or a summer storm will certainly damage them.

In Victorian times small fuchsias, especially the decorative leaf sorts, were planted out in borders as massed bedding plants, and standard fuchsias of a contrasting colour were often placed as dot plants among them. Unfortunately these massed bedding schemes are rarely seen today.

The non-hardy fuchsias, which are often only temporary inhabitants of the garden, can be planted in full sun, but the pale-coloured cultivars especially will also give a surprisingly good performance in light shade. In all cases the plants can stay in their original containers, though it is better if they are planted directly in the soil. At the end of the season they can be dug up, long roots trimmed back, and be potted up again and returned to the greenhouse for the winter.

In a hot summer all fuchsias grow better in a garden environment, as even the best greenhouse will then become difficult to manage and the atmosphere will be too hot and dry for them. A useful asset of outdoor fuchsias is that they will also thrive in a wet summer, in contrast to most other flowering plants which often dislike continually wet weather.

4
Training Fuchsias

A certain amount of training is advisable for any fuchsia. The removal of the growing tips in the early stages of growth will not only improve the shape and bushiness of the plant but will also increase the amount of flower it can ultimately produce. The shaping of the plant during active growth is often called summer pruning.

The bush form

This is the most usual and basic shape in which to train a fuchsia. The process starts when the growing tip is removed (i.e. pinched out) from a young plant which has about four to six pairs of well developed leaves. This young plant will then develop branches from each leaf axil. Each of these new shoots should have the tips removed when they have produced three pairs of leaves. For a general decorative effect this amount of training is usually sufficient, but a further improvement can be made by continuing to pinch out the tips as they grow. At a late stage, exhibitors will often pinch each stem after it has produced only one or two pairs of leaves. Each time the plant is stopped (pinched out) the formation of blooms will be delayed, so a natural time limit will be imposed on the shaping process if a full season's flowering is to be realized.

As the plant begins to mature it will be necessary to provide thin canes and judiciously placed ties to support the main branches. Each cultivar is an individual and it will tax the ingenuity of the grower to train it to the desired

Opposite:
'Annabel' (see page 84) trained as a standard

Left:
Training a bush fuchsia. When the stem of a young plant has grown four to six pairs of leaves it should have the growing tip removed (1) to encourage the side shoots to develop. A further pinch after the stems have grown to three or four pairs of leaves should produce a sufficiently bushy plant for ordinary decorative purposes (2)

shape. There is no limit to the ultimate size of the plant except that imposed by the space available and the vigour of the cultivar.

THE STANDARD FORM

This form is only a bush plant which has been trained at the top of a long stem. Standards are grown in three main size categories – table, half, and full. The table standard has a bare stem measured from soil level to the first branch of between 25 and 43 cm (10 and 17 in); the stems of a half and full standard measure 46–73 cm (18–29 in) and 76–106 cm (30–42 in) respectively.

It is worth making a special selection of cuttings which are to be grown on for standards. In a batch of cuttings, one or two will often stand out as stronger than the others, and these will be particularly good plants to choose for the purpose. Some cuttings will produce leaves in threes instead of the more usual pairs, and it will be easier to form a good symmetrical head on standards grown from these.

The selected cutting is potted up in the usual manner and tied to a short cane,

A standard fuchsia is produced by tieing a sturdy young plant to a cane (1) and removing the side shoots as they form (2). The latter process is best carried out by carefully tearing the shoots from the plant with a sideways movement rather than pinching them out (3). When the standard has reached nearly the required height the growing tip should be pinched out, leaving the top three or four sets of side shoots to develop (4). Note that the supporting cane should project well into the head of the developing plant and as it continues to grow it is tied at approximately 5 cm (2 in) intervals. Each side shoot is removed as soon as it is big enough to handle, by holding it between the thumb and forefinger where it joins the stem and pulling it sideways with the other hand until it breaks cleanly away. When an unwanted shoot is removed in this way it is less likely to regrow from the same point. All the leaves must be retained along the length of the main stem until the head is well formed or the whip, as the plant is called at this stage, will not grow properly. The young standard is re-potted and given a longer cane whenever necessary, and there must be no check to growth at any stage. The stem of the young whip will probably be quite thin at this stage; it will gradually thicken in proportion to supply the needs of the standard as the head enlarges. A greenhouse heated to 13°C (55°F) is an advantage as the growth must take place in a continuous operation to avoid forming a kink in the stem. It is also advantageous if the main growth is made in winter, when the chance of flowering is much reduced.

When the whip has reached almost the desired height the top four sets of side shoots are allowed to remain and the tip of the main stem is pinched out. These branches are the nucleus of the head of the standard, which is then trained in the same way as the bush form. The ultimate size of the head of the standard must always be in proportion to the rest of the plant. To retain this balance the head should be pruned back by two thirds at the end of each season and regrown the following year. The supporting cane should extend well into the head of the plant and ties should be made from it to carry the weight of all of the main branches.

A list of recommended cultivars especially suitable for growing as standards is given at the end of this book. Even if a hardy cultivar is grown as a standard it could be subject to severe damage in cold weather, and must be grown under protection in winter.

THE HANGING BASKET

This is not really a specially trained form of the fuchsia but rather a way of growing the plant in a special position. Any cultivar whose growth tends to be low, horizontal or trailing will make a good choice for a hanging basket, and this is also a good way of displaying the flowers to their best effect.

A certain amount of early stopping, in the manner described for the bush form, will greatly improve the appearance of the finished basket. One big plant is usually sufficient for a medium sized container, but three or even five or more smaller plants can be used to fill a large one. Hanging baskets are made of galvanized or plastic-coated wire, or are constructed entirely of plastic. The wire baskets, which are made in a variety of sizes, will have to be lined with moss, plastic sheeting or one of the special liners sold for the purpose. The all-plastic baskets, which are, at the time of writing, only made in sizes up to 30 cm (12 in) in diameter, need no lining and usually have the convenience of a built-in drip tray.

The actual planting of the basket is largely a matter of common sense. A single plant must be placed in the centre of the container, but if several smaller plants are used they should be placed in such a manner that they evenly fill the basket. If a very pendent cultivar is chosen it will be necessary to place an extra one in the middle of the basket to avoid having a bare centre. An advantage of the wire type of container is that small plants can be inserted between the wires and around the bottom and sides of the basket, thus creating a complete ball shape. Established hanging baskets need a great deal of watering, and regular weekly or twice weekly feeding will be required.

In these demanding conditions a John Innes No.3 compost will be found to give best results. If a hanging basket is planted up in February and grown on at a temperature of 13°C (55°F), and only stopped once, it will flower from early summer onwards. It is always better to use a single cultivar to each basket as different sorts will grow at different rates, giving a misshapen, ugly effect.

Opposite: 'Phyllis' (see page 105) trained as a standard

Right: 'Spion Kop' (see page 109) trained as a bush

Planting up a hanging basket. Wire baskets must be lined with moss or some other liner before being planted up (1). Place a piece of plastic sheeting over the top of the moss lining before adding potting compost and planting up (2). This will help to conserve moisture and reduce maintenance. Make a few holes in the plastic sheeting near the bottom of the basket to allow excess water to drain away, and trim the top of the sheet level with the top of the moss.

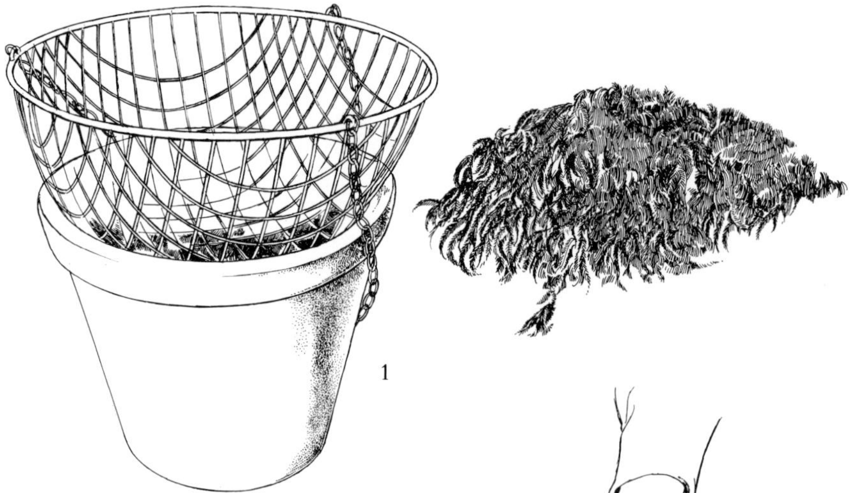

1

2

3

A solid plastic basket with a built-in drip tray needs no lining

THE PILLAR OR CORDON

This form is produced when a single stem is trained up a supporting cane, as described under growing standards, but all the side shoots are retained instead of pinching them out. The true pillar has all the side branches trimmed to the same length, so the finished plant looks like a tall cylinder. In practice it is often easier to allow the lower branches to grow longer than the higher ones, giving the plant a tapered appearance.

The pillar or cordon system of training requires all the side shoots to be retained (1). The plant should be tied at regular intervals to a supporting cane as it grows. The side branches are neatly trimmed (2)

THE PYRAMID

In its ideal shape the outline of this form is rather like a equilateral triangle, and the difficulty in its training is to encourage the lower branches to grow to a suitable length. A carefully selected, vigorous young cutting is grown as a single stem, but with all side branches retained, and tied to a supporting cane. When the plant reaches a certain height the growing tip is removed, allowing much of the vigour to be diverted to the side branches. One of the strongest side shoots is chosen from near the top of the plant and is carefully tied to the supporting stake, thus providing a new leading growth.

This procedure is repeated until the required height is reached. During the training process the point at which the growing tip is pinched out will depend on

'Display' (see page 92) trained as a pillar, a striking variation on the standard fuchsia form

Far left: 'Harry Gray' (see page 97) is well suited to hanging baskets

Left: 'Eva Boerg' (see page 93) is best trained as a bush

Left: A single plant of 'Sophisticated Lady' (see page 109) in a hanging basket. It took three years to develop this cascade of flowers

Fuchsia splendens
(see page 82)

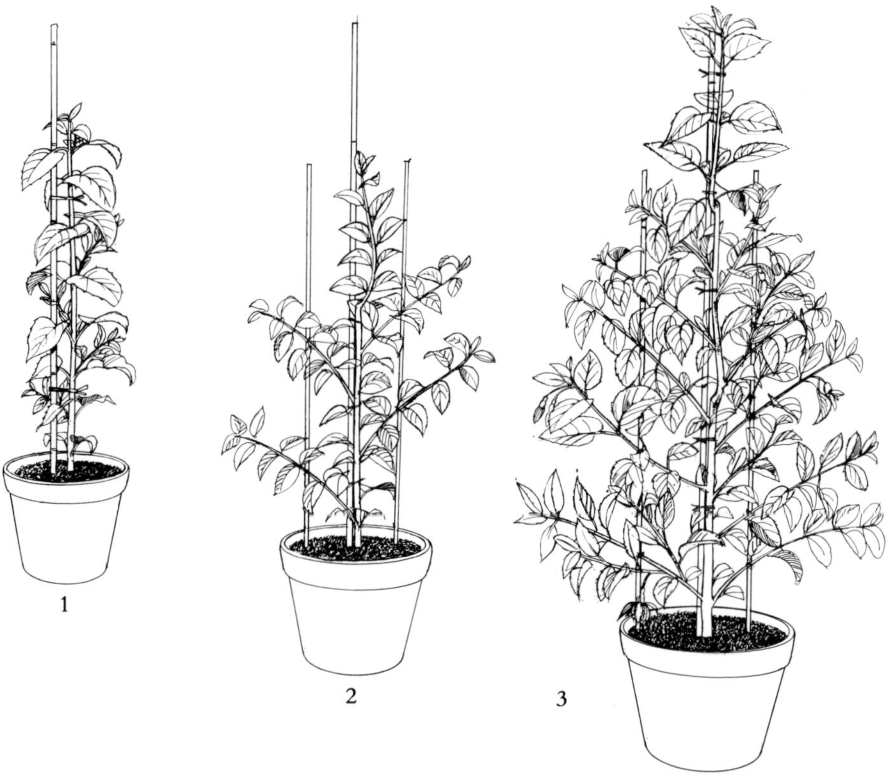

Training a pyramid involves growing a single stem with side shoots intact (1). The tip is pinched out and a strong side shoot is selected to form the new leader (2). The vigorous growth of the side shoots means that they need support in addition to that provided for the main stem (3)

the cultivar being used and the opinion of the grower, but for best results it should be done at any time when the plant reaches between 15 and 45 cm (6 and 18 in) in height, and subsequently at similar intervals. Most of the branches must be well supported or they will certainly break off when weighed down with flowers. This form is considered the most difficult to grow and master, and it will take at least two years to grow a good specimen pyramid. The first year will involve growing the plant up to its final height, and at least another year's growth will be needed to perfect the outline shape of the plant. Extra tall specimens up to 3 m (9 or 10 ft) in height will take proportionally longer to grow.

ESPALIERS, FANS AND CLIMBERS

These specialized forms were all popular in the past, but like the pyramid form they are rarely met with today as the necessary time and space involved in growing them precludes their culture. They are occasionally still seen at some of the major flower shows or on display in the large greenhouses of botanical gardens or public parks.

5
Propagation

The fuchsia is an easy plant to propagate, and with suitable modifications to technique cuttings can be taken at any time of year. The natural cycle of growth means that there is a wide variation in the nature of the shoots available for propagation, though the basic principles involved are always the same. The advice given here on the selection and preparation of the cutting material is divided according to the seasons. It is mainly concerned with plants growing in the greenhouse. Cuttings can also be taken from plants growing in the garden, but propagation material obtained from this source will inevitably be behind the schedules outlined below, and an allowance must be made accordingly.

Spring

At this time the plants are beginning to grow strongly again after a period of slow growth or dormancy in winter. There should not, at this stage, be any signs of flower buds forming. When the new shoots have reached 4–5 cm (1½–2 in) in length, the end 2.5–4 cm (1–1½ in) is cut off using a very sharp knife or razor blade, leaving approximately 1 cm (½ in) remaining on the plant. The two lower leaves are removed, and the cutting is ready to be inserted (see illustrations on page 60). It is unimportant whether the cutting is taken immediately below a leaf axil or not, as either type will root easily at this time of year. A hormone rooting powder is not essential as this type of cutting will root easily without it, but a preparation containing a fungicide such as Captan can sometimes protect the cutting from rotting.

At this time of year and for optimum results a soil temperature in the region of 18°C (64°F) is necessary, so some form of greenhouse propagator should be used to reduce heating costs. Under optimum conditions progress is rapid and rooting will be well advanced in seven to ten days. If access to a simple propagator or heated bed is not possible, or if the stock plants from which the cuttings are to be taken are not sufficiently advanced, the cuttings are best taken later in the year; alternatively, they can be rooted on a windowsill in a warm house.

Summer

Once the new shoots produced in the spring have enlarged and started to show flower buds, cuttings taken from them will root more slowly and the losses will be greater. Flowering occurs when the level of various hormones within the plant changes, and this process unfortunately also slows down vegetative growth and the production of roots.

Cuttings taken during the summer will need to be longer than those taken in the spring: shoot tips approximately 6–8 cm (2½–3 in) long are ideal. The lowest pair or two pairs of leaves are removed and the lower end of the cutting is trimmed to just below a leaf node; any flower buds should be removed as they

Opposite: 'Thalia' (see page 112)

Provided that suitable conditions can be given, fuchsias can be rooted at any time of the year. However, small, soft tip cuttings from young, non-flowering shoots in the spring are preferred, as they root more quickly and reliably than other types of cutting.

spring cutting

summer cutting

autumn cutting with a heel

will continue to grow and weaken the cutting. A hormone rooting powder should be used for this type of cutting.

In the summer no extra heating or special apparatus is required for rooting purposes, and many amateur growers choose the warmer months for propagating their favourite plants. This is the basis of the so-called biennial method, where plants are propagated in one year to mature and flower the next season. This system has the advantage that the plants that need to be carried through the winter are relatively small, but will produce large specimens for the next year. Many exhibitors prefer to take summer cuttings because of this.

Autumn

The weather in early autumn is often almost the same as in late summer; the type of cutting material obtained and its treatment is also the same at this time, but later in the autumn the plants will produce semi-hardwood, non-flowering cuttings. These cuttings, which can be any length up to a maximum of about 12 cm (7 in), are torn off the stock plant so as to form a heel, the lower leaves are removed and the cutting is dipped in hormone rooting powder and inserted in the usual manner.

Cuttings taken in this way are slow to root. They will often lose their leaves during the winter, and will not start to show new growth until the following spring. These cuttings must be kept at a minimum temperature of 7°C (45°F) throughout the cold weather or they will probably die.

Winter

In early winter, semi-hardwood cuttings can be taken as described for the autumn period. As they are unlikely to root until spring they must also be kept at a minimum temperature of 7°C (45°F). Depending on the temperature maintained, in late winter young cuttings of new growth become available, and these are treated in the same manner as spring cuttings.

General procedures

One of the most important principles involved in plant propagation is to take cuttings only from the very best plants. The potential mother plants should be carefully selected for freedom from disease and for their vigour, quantity and quality of flower, and whether they are typical examples of the particular species or cultivar. The cuttings taken from such plants will perpetuate these desirable characteristics. It is a mistake to raise a number of plants for display or exhibition and to use the misshapen failures for propagation. This will probably reduce the quality of next season's specimens and cause a gradual decline in the quality of the collection.

After the cuttings have been selected and prepared as described, they are ready for planting. As soon as they have been inserted they should be thoroughly watered overhead with a fungicide containing benomyl or iprodione to prevent formation of botrytis (grey mould), which is encouraged by the close, humid conditions required for rooting.

The choice of rooting medium is a matter of personal preference, but it is important to use a compost or other material which is specially formulated for the purpose, or results can be very disappointing. Ordinary potting composts usually contain a high level of fertilizer, which will inhibit good root formation in the early stages of growth. Soilless seed sowing or cutting composts generally give best results, but John Innes cutting compost, if available, works well.

The cuttings can be planted a few inches apart in trays, or a smaller number can be planted round the edge of a pot. Small individual containers or partitioned trays in which single plants can be rooted have always been popular with commercial growers, and many are now available to the amateur. The advantage of the small individual containers is that the plants raised in them can be transplanted with the minimum of root disturbance, and they will grow away more quickly when potted on.

Cuttings can also be inserted in other materials such as vermiculite or perlite, which can either be used alone or admixed with an equal volume of moss peat. These materials contain no fertilizer at all, and it is vital that cuttings rooted in this way are moved into a normal potting compost as soon as possible to avoid a check in growth.

Opposite: 'Preston Guild' (see page 107)

Below: 'Cloverdale Pearl' (see page 90)

Cuttings may be planted individually or several together round the edges of a pot. Water them in with a fungicidal solution immediately after insertion into the compost, and then keep them in a moist atmosphere out of direct sunlight. Newly planted cuttings must not be allowed to wilt excessively or they will not survive

The small, softwood cuttings available in the late winter and spring are often preferred as they tend to root very easily, but they also have a tendency to wilt, particularly in hot, dry weather. If this process occurs it will seriously impair the ability of the cutting to root, and it is of paramount importance to take all steps possible to prevent excessive wilting. In hot weather, plants intended for propagation should be kept well watered, and as soon as the cuttings are taken they should be dropped into a container partly filled with water. This will ensure that they do not deteriorate before being inserted into the rooting medium. Once the cuttings have been planted it is still necessary to take every precaution to prevent wilting, and in summer a minimum of a 50 per cent reduction in the light level will be required. They will also need to be enclosed in a propagating case or some sort of transparent or translucent tent to provide a close, humid atmosphere. Individual pots can be enclosed in polythene bags to provide the correct micro-climate around the cuttings. Do not forget to enclose a suitable label with each batch of plants. These special conditions apply mostly to spring and summer cuttings; the more woody cuttings taken in the late autumn and winter are generally given open greenhouse conditions from the start.

When the plants are well rooted they should be uncovered as soon as possible, but the shading must be retained for a few more days until they have become accustomed to the drier air. Cuttings that have rooted can, with a little practice, be recognized by their healthy, turgid appearance, which is quite different from the dull look of a cutting that has failed to root. Once the young plants are fully rooted and are showing signs of new growth, they should be potted up before there is any check to growth, as this can seriously affect the future potential of the plant.

Although the use of a greenhouse or similar facility is desirable, it is still possible to propagate fuchsia plants entirely in the open. Semi-hardwood cuttings are best for this purpose; they can be found on outdoor plants in mid to late summer. The ideal cutting would be about 10 cm (4 in) from the tip to where it joins the main branch. This junction will probably be beginning to turn brown as the wood begins to mature. The cutting is torn off the main branch leaving a small heel at the base of the stem. A few of the lower leaves and any flower buds are removed, and the base of the cutting is dipped in hormone rooting powder and then either inserted directly in the open ground near the mother plant or placed in a small container that can be sited in a shady position elsewhere in the garden. The cuttings should be watered after they are planted and rewatered as necessary in dry weather. A number of such cuttings should be taken, as losses can be high.

The plants will be well rooted in autumn, and they can either be dug up and given winter protection under glass or, in the case of the hardy cultivars, can be heavily mulched with peat and allowed to remain in position until the spring. When new growth appears the young plants can be carefully removed and replanted into their final position.

Hybridization and seed sowing

There are two basic methods for producing new fuchsia hybrids. The first is by sowing seed produced by cross-pollination of two different plants. Because of the complex ancestry of many fuchsias the nature of the resulting seedlings is often unpredictable, and their character can be unlike that of either of the parents. The second method is by natural mutation (sporting), which will produce a flower of a different colour, or perhaps a plant with variegated leaves. This process is generally beyond the grower's control; mutations can be induced by the use of radiation or certain dangerous chemicals such as colchicine, but such techniques are outside the scope of the average amateur gardener.

Occasionally a natural mutation will be found on an otherwise normal plant, and if this part with altered leaf or flower colour is allowed to grow and develop several cuttings can be taken from it. When rooted and grown on to maturity these cuttings should still have the character of the new variety or cultivar.

Seed can be obtained either from a seedsman or from the grower's own plants by a process of deliberate crossing, or by harvesting the fertile berries that have been pollinated by bees. Sowing instructions are given on professionally packeted seeds, and these should be followed carefully; do not expect high germination – a 30 per cent rate is often all that can be realized.

Before hand pollination is undertaken, the nature of the proposed crosses must be considered. There should always be a specific object or improvement in mind, and the actual choice of parent plants will reflect this aim. A frequently used principle in plant breeding is to use two parents each of which have separate desirable characteristics, in the hope that some of these features will be inherited together in one of the offspring. The course that any breeding programme should follow can be predicted by the laws of heredity, which were discovered in the nineteenth century by Gregor Mendel. The detailed principles involved in plant breeding are complex and beyond the scope of this book, but readers who wish to pursue the matter further should consult a specialist work on plant breeding and genetics.

The actual process of cross-pollination is relatively simple (see illustration on page 68). An unopen but nearly mature flower bud is chosen on the intended mother plant. The bud is opened by gently squeezing it, after which the sepals are peeled back. This will reveal the unripe anthers and stigma. The anthers (pollen-bearing parts) are removed by cutting through the filaments with a pair of pointed scissors to prevent self-pollination, and the flower is then enclosed in a soft paper bag to prevent access by insects. The stigma will not be receptive at this stage but it will become mature in two or three days. When this happens, ripe

Opposite: Because fuchsias grow so well in containers they can enhance the smallest garden or porch all summer long

Right: 'Buttercup' (see page 88)

pollen from the chosen male plant should be smeared over it; if the pollen does not stick, the stigma is still not sufficiently receptive.

This process should be repeated on a number of flowers. The fruits will ripen in two to four months, and the small seed is found by picking through the soft, juicy flesh of the berries. The number of seeds contained in each berry will vary considerably, and the numbers obtained are often very small. The seed, which is on average only about 1 mm across, should be sown as soon as possible after harvesting. Any recognized seed compost will be suitable, and the seed should only be barely covered. At a temperature of 16°C (60°F) it will start to germinate in about two weeks, and then should be pricked out and grown on like any other plant. Seed sown in late summer will, if the resulting plants are grown on at 13°C (55°F), flower the following year.

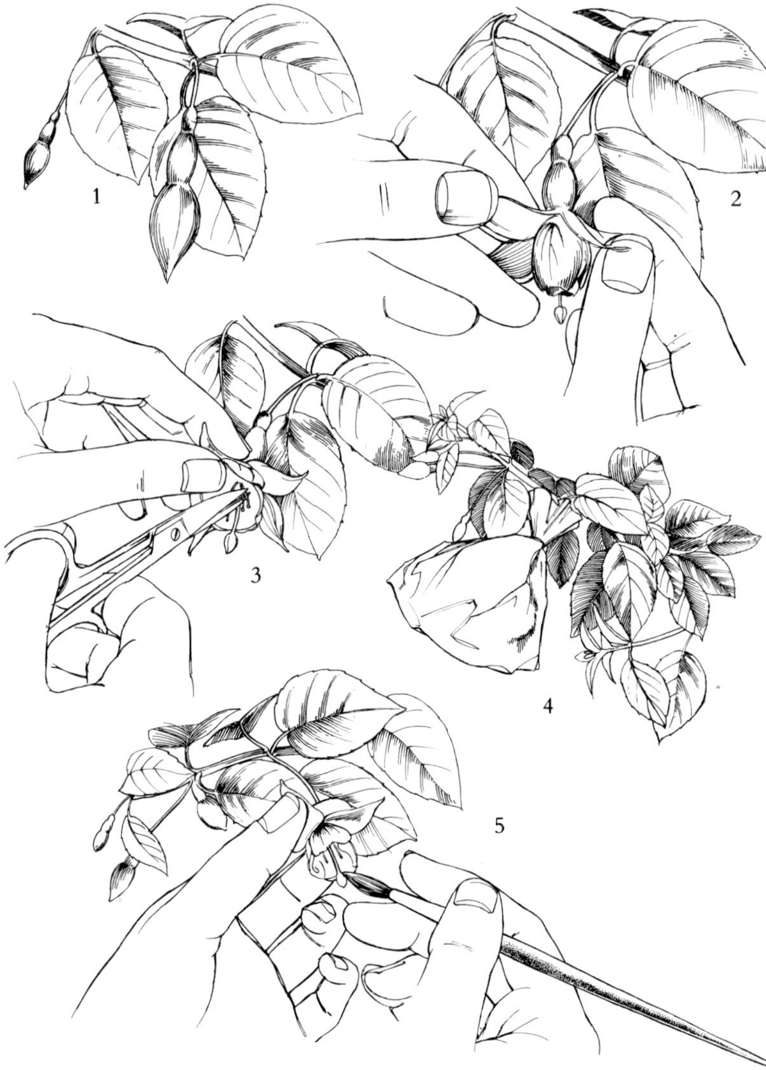

Pollinating a fuchsia. To prevent unwanted self-pollination by insects the immature flower bud (1) must be opened (2), emasculated (3) and protected by a paper bag (4) until the stigma is ripe and ready to receive pollen from the other chosen parent (5). Remember to replace the paper bag until the flower dies.

6
Pests and Diseases

The fuchsia is not beset by many troublesome pests and diseases, but there are nevertheless various problems to watch out for. The most common pests of fuchsias are aphids, whiteflies and spider mites. Fuchsia rust and botrytis (grey mould) are the two fungal diseases most likely to occur. Early prevention is much more effective than tackling an established outbreak of disease with a whole armoury of chemicals. Problems like the regular occurrence of whiteflies can be anticipated and protective sprays applied in good time. General greenhouse hygiene and annual sterilization of materials and staging plays a vital part in combating disease. The removal of weeds and debris from around the plants will prevent reinfection once an outbreak has occurred.

Many chemical insecticides are very effective, but they are often toxic to human beings and beneficial insects alike, and must be used according to the manufacturer's instructions. Usually, when used as directed, wet sprays and smoke generators are equally effective. The smoke cones or tablets are often quicker and less troublesome to use than the equivalent sprays, but they are generally more expensive. Aerosol spray cans are also a convenient but expensive way of buying chemicals. Fuchsias are sensitive to some gardening products and the list of exclusions on the labels should be checked carefully for this information before purchase. Chemical sprays should always be applied in the evening, or on a dull, sunless day, or damage to the plants can occur even with a normally safe product. There are several brands of proprietary insecticides that contain more than one active ingredient, and these will effectively control a wide range of pests. These mixtures are a labour-saving way of giving a broad spectrum of protection with one spray, which can be an important feature if the damaging pest cannot be identified.

The names of the chemicals mentioned in this book are the active ingredients of the preparation. Manufacturers will often market their products under different brand names, although the active substance, which will be listed in the small print on the container, is often the same. New chemicals are always being introduced onto the market so the grower should always be prepared to try promising new products as they become available.

Many growers, for good reasons, dislike the use of chemical sprays; biological methods of control are now available for most of the common pests. Sources of supply for these products are advertised from time to time in the pages of specialist gardening magazines, and can also be obtained on request (accompanied by a stamped addressed envelope) from the appropriate gardening adviser of the publication.

Pests

Aphids (greenfly) These are small, mostly wingless insects (their life cycle is complex, and winged forms occur at certain times of year) which can be green or bluish in colour. They suck sap, and heavy infestations of them can excrete copious amounts of honeydew formed from surplus sugars in the sap and on which black, sooty moulds can grow. The moulds are not in themselves harmful to the plant, but are very unsightly. Various products are effective against aphids, including those containing dimethoate, gamma HCH, malathion and diazinon.

Whitefly (*Trialeurodes vaporariorum*) Adult whitefly have the appearance of minute white moths which make short,often spiralling, flights when disturbed. In its juvenile stage the whitefly appears as a small, scale-like creature attached to the undersides of the leaves. This scale protects the larva within from contact with insecticides. Sooty moulds will grow on the excretions of these insects. Fortunately, synthetic analogues of pyrethrum, a naturally occurring insecticide, are very effective and are relatively non-poisonous to human beings. The best product to use is one containing permethrin; when used as directed this will be found to be a good means of controlling this troublesome pest. Two or three applications at ten-day intervals may be necessary in order to clear the infestation completely, catching the young whitefly after they emerge and before they can breed. Alternatively, the introduction of the parasitic wasp *Encarsia* will give good biological control.

Spider mite (*Tetranychus urticae*) This pest is very common and causes speckling and bronzing of the leaves, and sometimes premature leaf fall. The tiny mites, which are almost indiscernible to the naked eye, spin fine webs, especially on the undersides of the leaves. This can be a difficult pest to eradicate as it has become resistant to many insecticides. Although many manufacturers recommend the use of their product for the control of spider mites, most insecticides such as malathion and dimethoate are now of little use. There are a number of effective products, but at the moment these are unfortunately only available to professional growers. However, a well grown fuchsia will outgrow this pest, and the practice of strict hygiene in the greenhouse will prevent the hibernating mites from surviving from one season to the next. If chemical methods fail, the introduction of the predatory mite *Phytoseilus persimilis* will give good biological control in greenhouses.

Capsid bug (*Lygocoris pabulinus*) These are active yellow-green insects, which mainly attack outdoor plants. They feed on the young leaves, which eventually become deformed and tattered with irregular holes. The cure is to spray with an insecticide containing gamma HCH.

Caterpillars Occasionally the elephant hawk moth (*Deilephila elpenor*) will lay its eggs on fuchsias. The adult caterpillars are huge, up to 7.5 cm (3 in) in length. The adult moth is a very beautiful insect, and as it is uncommon it is hoped that the grower will overlook the occasional trouble caused by this insect and let it survive.

Opposite: Out of doors, fuchsias combine well with other shrubs. On the whole they are trouble-free but keep a watch out for capsid bug and caterpillar damage

Sciarids The adults are small black flies, but it is the soilborne larvae which cause the damage, generally only to seedlings or cuttings. They can be controlled by stirring a little gamma HCH powder into the surface of the soil around the

infected plants. Sciarids particularly favour soilless composts which have been overwatered.

Vine weevil (*Otiorhynchus sulcatus*) This is a potentially very damaging pest, and they are an increasing problem. The creamy-white larvae have brown heads and can be over 1.5 cm ($\frac{1}{2}$ in) long. They eat the stems, roots and leaves and often cause the whole plant to wilt or die. These insects can be deterred by stirring a little gamma HCH dust into the surface of the soil, but unfortunately they are very difficult to eradicate completely.

Cyclamen mite, **leaf hoppers** and **thrips** have also been recorded as causing damage to fuchsias. Spraying with an insecticide containing gamma HCH or diazinon will prove effective against all of them.

DISEASES

Fuchsia rust (*Pucciniastrum epilobi*) This disease is characterized by the raised, round, bright rust coloured spots on the undersides of the leaves. All infected parts must be removed and burned. The plants should be sprayed with a fungicide containing thiram, maneb or zineb at fortnightly intervals, or until the problem disappears. Oxycarboxin is another product which is particularly effective, but at the present time it is only available to professional growers. This disease is also harboured by relatives of the fuchsia such as willow herbs, and to prevent reinfection these weeds should be removed from the vicinity of the greenhouse and garden.

Botrytis (grey mould, *Botrytis cinerea*) The name grey mould is very descriptive of this disease. Affected leaves and stems become covered with a downy mass of grey spores. Cold, damp and stagnant air favours the growth of the fungus. Plenty of ventilation, when possible, and the use of heat will help to control the disease. Spraying with fungicides containing benomyl or iprodione, or fumigating with tecnazene smokes, should prove beneficial, but unfortunately there are many resistant strains of this disease.

Black mould This harmless fungus grows on the surface of leaves where the nectar from flowers has fallen. It is unsightly and can prove difficult to remove. The affected plants can be stood in the open and rainfall will eventually clear away the problem. (See also under *Aphids* and *Whitefly*.)

PHYSIOLOGICAL AND OTHER DISORDERS

Leaf drop A certain amount of leaf drop is normal in the autumn, and leaves often become blotched with yellow before they fall. Leaves and flower buds on certain sensitive cultivars will also fall in unsuitably hot and dry conditions. A severe attack of spider mites will also cause leaf drop.

Leaf discoloration As already stated, a certain amount of leaf discoloration and fall is normal in the autumn, even from plants growing in a heated greenhouse.

Parts of the leaf will remain green at first, but various yellow, brown and purple spots begin to spread. This can look alarming but should only affect the older leaves, and it is due to the natural changes taking place within the plant when the days become shorter. A purple tinge to the leaves in summer, especially on purple or deep red flowered sorts, is often due to incipient nitrogen starvation, and a high nitrogen feed should be applied accordingly. Sunburn can also leave brown marks with purple edges on affected leaves.

Wilting Plants that have been grown under glass in winter and early spring are, because of lack of light, rather soft in growth. When a bright, warm day arrives and the ventilators are opened wide, the plants will often wilt even though the soil is nicely moist. There is usually nothing wrong with such plants, and when they become accustomed to the change in atmospheric conditions they quickly recover and behave normally.

Attacks by root-eating insects and minor root damage caused by overwatering or overfeeding will also cause a plant to wilt in warm weather. Severe cases of root damage can lead to excessive wilting, which will in turn cause the eventual death of the plant.

7
Fuchsia Calendar

Spring

This is the season when plants start to grow again after a partial or complete rest in winter. The final pruning or trimming of last season's growth should be carried out now. Remove all weak stems completely, together with any dead wood, and ensure that the plant has a neat and shapely appearance.

This is an excellent time to repot large plants, as any accidental damage to the root system will soon be made good. Young plants should be potted on into larger containers before their growth is checked. It is important to water newly potted fuchsias very carefully, because the roots can easily be damaged at this stage. Regular mist spraying with clean water is also very helpful to the plants. Even those specimens that have lost all their leaves during dormancy will benefit from regular spraying, as it softens the bark of the old stems and encourages the formation of new shoots.

When the stems have formed three or four new pairs of leaves the tip should be pinched out to promote bushiness. On average this process should be repeated only once or twice more. Although the shape of the plant will be improved by further pruning it will also delay flowering.

Short, sturdy new shoots can be used as cuttings to replace or increase stocks of any cultivar. Provided that suitable conditions can be given, cuttings will root more quickly at this time than in any other season and they will grow large enough to flower in the same year.

In cold climates hanging baskets can be planted up in the greenhouse and grown on to flowering size before being hardened off and used for outdoor decoration in the summer.

Keep a good look out for any signs of pests and diseases, and treat them promptly or they will rapidly multiply in warm weather and cause serious damage later on.

Shade the greenhouse to prevent the internal temperature from rising too high.

Summer

This is the main flowering season, so all pinching or pruning should cease except for rooted cuttings or those plants being trained for standards, pillars, etc. Large-flowering plants will require regular feeding, and if they need to be watered more than once a day they should be potted on into larger containers. When the plants are in full flower they should be fed with a high nitrogen fertilizer to stimulate growth. This will encourage to flower continuously some cultivars that would otherwise flower only in flushes. The removal of berries from the old flowers will help to promote more blooms and prolong the flowering season.

Cuttings can still be taken, and they will grow into good sized specimens for

Opposite: 'Prosperity' (see page 107)

display or exhibition the following year. Continue to mist spray the plants with fresh water, but discontinue the process if it starts to mark the open flowers. In periods of hot weather ensure that the atmosphere in the greenhouse is kept moist by frequently damping down around the plants and along pathways. In very hot conditions (above 27°C, 80°F) the plants will grow much better if they are moved out of doors into a slightly shaded position.

In late spring or early summer hardy plants in the garden will start to show new growth. Old, dead stems should be pruned away and a good dressing of a complete fertilizer sprinkled around the base of each plant. Hardy cultivars that are to be left permanently in the garden must be planted no later than mid summer so that they can become well established before the onset of cold weather. Continue to examine plants regularly for signs of disease, especially red spider mite, and treat accordingly.

Plants that are being trained as standards, pillars, etc. should not be allowed to flower; any buds that are formed should be picked off at an early stage. This will help to direct the energy of the plant into producing more stem growth rather than flowers that are not wanted at this time.

Autumn

Plants that are grown permanently out of doors in areas of frost will be in peak flower during the late summer and autumn. These plants will need little attention apart from ensuring that they are not attacked by insect pests, and keeping them well watered in prolonged dry periods. Tender plants that have been used for temporary decoration in the garden should be lifted before the first severe frost and the roots and stems trimmed before they are repotted and returned to the greenhouse for the winter.

As the temperature begins to fall the atmosphere will become more humid and fungal diseases such as grey mould (*Botrytis cinerea*) become more common. Old and decaying leaves and flowers should be removed or they may spread disease to the stems. A routine spray of a combined fungicide and insecticide can be very beneficial as it will help to reduce the population of pests and diseases that would otherwise overwinter and cause problems the following year.

Check the greenhouse structure and the functioning of the heaters, and make any repairs that are necessary. Electrical and gas appliances should only be serviced by qualified engineers.

Winter

Hardy fuchsias that have been planted in the previous summer should have the soil drawn up to the main stems, and a diameter of 30 cm (12 in) around the crown of each plant covered with a 5 cm (2 in) layer of coarse peat or similar material. This will give the plants added protection in the first critical winter

Plants in the greenhouse should be watered sparingly during the winter, the exact amount depending on the temperature that is being maintained. To minimize the spread of fungal diseases, remove dead or decaying leaves at

Fuchsia procumbens (see page 81), an unusual hardy species

frequent intervals and open the greenhouse ventilators whenever outside conditions allow. Insect pests should not be much of a problem, but hungry mice can cause considerable damage by chewing plant stems or electric cables.

Ensure that the temperature in the greenhouse does not fall below an absolute minimum of 1°C (34°F). Remember that some hybrids and species will not tolerate less than 7–10°C (45–50°F). A recording (maximum–minimum) thermometer is essential to ensure that excessively low temperatures are not reached during the night.

Cuttings can also be taken in late winter from the earliest of the new shoots. These cuttings are particularly useful for growing on as standards or other trained forms that require a lengthy period of continuous growth.

A to Z of Fuchsias

'Jeane' (see page 98) is frequently listed under the name 'Genii'

To save space and enable as many cultivars as possible to be included in this list, the following system of abbreviations has been adopted.

H – Hardy; can be grown out of doors without protection except in areas that are subject to severe or prolonged frost. These plants have usually been given an award for hardiness by the Royal Horticultural Society or are on an approved list produced by the British Fuschia Society.

S – Can easily be trained as a standard. Many of these cultivars will also be suitable for other trained forms, such as pyramids and pillars, etc.

B – Suitable for cultivation in hanging pots or baskets. If this is the only code letter given, the cultivar is probably so pendulous in its habit of growth that the use of any other type of container is impracticable.

P – Suitable for growing in pots, usually in a bush-trained form. Where the classifications **B** and **P** are given together it signifies that the cultivar in question has an intermediate form of growth which, with proper attention, can be cultivated in either type of container.

The descriptions of the flower colours mentioned in the text are typical of the plants concerned, but in practice they can vary with differences in cultural conditions. To avoid confusion the raiser of each cultivar, the date (where known) and the country where the hybrid originated is given in case the same name has been used for different hybrids. For example, apart from 'Constellation', the double white cultivar that is in general cultivation, there are also at least two other fuchsias with the same name. The date stated after the raiser's name is the earliest record known for that particular plant, either in a commercial nursery catalogue or its registration by the American Fuchsia Society. In the case of the species, the names and dates refer back to the earliest known descriptions of these plants.

The addresses of many fuchsia nurserymen will be found by consulting the classified columns of any specialist gardening magazine. These suppliers will stock many of the cultivars and species mentioned in this section, but commercial availability varies considerably from year to year, so not all the hybrids mentioned will be obtainable at any particular time.

The fuchsias listed in this section are but a small proportion of the many thousands of hybrids recorded in the literature, but they are representative of all of the best forms and colours currently available.

Very recently two fuchsias ('Space Shuttle' and 'Ronald L. Lockerbie') have been produced whose flower colour has been described as yellow. Although they have not been thoroughly tested, the author's impression is that the claims are very optimistic, and no recommendations can be made at the present time.

Fuchsia Species

F. arborescens
Sims–Central America 1865
Large, almost laurel-like leaves with small lilac flowers in the form of panicles. In its native habitat it grows to the size of a small tree. It is better to plant it out in a cool greenhouse border rather than cultivating it in a pot.

F. bacillaris see page 85

F. boliviana
Carr–Bolivia, Peru and Argentina 1876
The long, narrow flowers are borne in clusters and are coloured in shades of red. The foliage is light green, and attractive berries are formed after flowering. Needs warmth for success. *F. corymbiflora alba* is now recognized as a white-tubed variant of *F. boliviana.* **P**

F. corymbiflora alba *see boliviana*

F. denticulata
Ruiz and Pavón–Peru and Bolivia 1802
This species is best grown in a heated greenhouse border. The long tube is a deep pink and the corolla an orange or red colour. It is commonly found listed under its synonym *F. serratifolia.*

F. excorticata
Forster–New Zealand 1776
The tube and sepals are green and purplish-red. The corolla is deep purple. The blue pollen and yellow stigma add to the charm of the small flowers. Hardy only in the mildest districts. **H**

F. fulgens
De Candolle–Mexico 1828
The long flowers are borne in terminal clusters. The flowers are orange-red with greenish-yellow sepals. This species has very large, hairy leaves and requires heat. There are a number of varieties of this species and all are worth growing.

F. magellanica
Lamarck–Argentina and Chile 1767
The typical plant has small red and purple flowers. This species is vigorous and bushy and can form small trees in milder areas. *F. magellanica* and many of its varieties and hybrids are among the most satisfactory and hardy of the garden fuchsias. *F. magellanica* var. *molinae* (var. *alba*) has very pale lilac flowers. Variety *pumila* has tiny scarlet and mauve flowers on a small plant which is suitable for rockeries. *F. magellanica* var. *gracilis* 'Variegata' (correctly, but less widely known as var. *macrostemma* 'Variegata') has variegated foliage. Many other varieties are available (see 'Tricolorii' page 113), all of which make excellent garden plants. **HP**

F. microphylla
Kris–Mexico 1823
The tiny flowers are produced from the leaf axils. The flower colour is variable but is typically red with a pink corolla. Small, dainty leaves. A small, upright shrub, hardy in most areas. **HP**

F. procumbens
Cunningham–New Zealand 1834
An unusual hardy plant suitable for rockeries. The leaves are very small and rounded, and the long, thin, woody stems creep across the ground. The flowers are small and point up-

Opposite: *Fuchsia denticulata* (see page 81)

Right: *Fuchsia procumbens* (see page 81)

wards, and are curiously coloured in shades of yellow, violet and green. The stamens are red and blue. The fruits are quite large and ripen to a plum purple colour. An interesting species and well worth growing. Synonymous with *F. prostrata*. **HP**

F. regia* var. *alpestris

Brazil

This variety is the plant most frequently met with in cultivation. The flowers are red and purple and similar to *F. magellanica* but not hardy. Often listed as *F. alpestris*. **P**

F. splendens

Zuccarini–Mexico to Costa Rica 1832

A beautiful species for greenhouse cultivation. The short tube is red with yellow-green tips. The corolla is a shade of yellow-green. The plant will make quite a large shrub but is more controllable and will flower better when confined to a pot. **P**

Fuchsia Cultivars

'Achievement'
Melville–Britain 1886. Single
The tube and sepals are red and the corolla is a bright purple colour. The flowers are quite large and are freely produced. An old cultivar which is still very popular. Upright growth. Very similar to 'Charming' and 'Goliath'. **SP**

'Alaska'
Schnabel–USA 1963. Double
Virtually pure white, the corolla is full and ruffled. Upright, rather spreading growth. **P**

'Alice Hoffman'
Klevse or Klese–Germany 1911. Semi-double
The tube and sepals are rose and the corolla milky white veined with red. The leaves are tinged with bronze. Compact, upright growth. **HP**

'Alison Ryle'
Ryle–Britain 1968. Semi-double
The sepals are pink and the corolla lilac-blue and mauve. Large flowers; upright growth. **P**

'Alyce Larson'
Tiret–USA 1972. Double
The tube is white and the sepals are white, tipped pink. Corolla pure white. Trailing growth. **BP**

'Ambassador'
Jones–Britain 1962. Single
The tube and sepals are white and pink. The corolla markedly changes colour with age from deep violet-purple to light purple. Strong, upright growth. **P**

'Angela Leslie'
Tiret–USA 1959. Double
The flower is in shades of pink throughout. The corolla is very full and veined in red. Large, very showy blooms. The upright growth needs support. **P**

'Angela Rippon'
Gadsby–Britain 1977. Single
The tube and sepals are a pale, waxy pink with green tinges. The corolla is mid blue. Very compact, upright and short-jointed growth. Very freely produced, medium sized flowers. **SP**

'Angel's Dream'
Stubbs–USA 1973. Double
The large flowers have a pink tube and sepals and a pink and white flared corolla. Very beautiful and free flowering. Arching growth. Similar to, but better than, 'Angel's Flight' and 'Beauty of Bath'. **SBP**

'Annabel'
Ryle–Britain 1977. Double
The large flowers can be pure white but are often tinged pink. The blooms are borne in great profusion on upright stems. Light green leaves. Similar to 'Igloo Maid' but in many respects better. This cultivar has great merit, and though fairly new is already an established favourite. **SP**

'Applause'
Stubbs–USA 1978. Double
Broad pink sepals with a white mid-stripe. The very large, spreading corolla, which in the United States is described as orange-red, tends to be a

pinkish-orange under British conditions – a bright and pleasing colour nonetheless. Arching growth. **BP**

'Army Nurse'
Hodges–USA 1947. Semi-double
The tube and sepals are deep red, the corolla bluish-violet. The small flowers are produced in profusion on an upright, vigorous plant. Not hardy in the most exposed areas. **HSP**

'Arthur Cope'
Gadsby–Britain 1968. Semi-double
The tube and sepals are pearly white. The corolla is bright red, dappled with white. Large, freely produced flowers on rather horizontal growth. **BP**

'Aunt Juliana'
Hanson–USA 1950. Double
Red tube and sepals; pale lavender-blue corolla veined with red. The large flowers are produced on lax stems. **B**

'Autumnale'
Meteor–Europe ?1880. Single
Scarlet sepals, purple corolla. The growth is made horizontally and the large golden leaves have a strong red/bronze flush. Medium sized flowers; very handsome. **B**

'Baby Pink'
Soo Yun–USA 1976. Double
The medium sized, palest pink flowers are produced in great profusion. Bushy growth. **BP**

F. × bacillaris
Mexico–F. microphylla × F. thymifolia
× Bacillaris is a group of first generation hybrids produced by crossing the two species. They form beautiful small shrubs with small crimson flowers. The hybrid 'Cottinghamii' is similar in appearance but slightly larger in growth. Both hybrids are reasonably hardy. **H**

'Barbara'
Tolley–Britain 1971. Single
A medium sized flower in two shades of pink. Growth is upright and exceedingly vigorous, but when brought under control this can be very effective as a show plant. **SP**

'Bella Forbes'
Forbes–Britain 1890. Double
The tube and sepals are red and the full corolla milky white. An old, large flowered cultivar which has stood the test of time. Upright growth. **SP**

'Belsay Beauty'
Ryle–Britain 1975. Semi-double
The medium sized flowers have pink sepals and a violet-blue corolla. The mid-green foliage is a perfect foil for the flowers. Upright, well branched growth. A superb cultivar, which like many singles is often ignored by the general public. **P**

'Bicentennial'
Paskesen–USA 1976. Double
The corolla has orange outer and magenta inner petals; pale orange sepals. The medium to large sized flowers are produced in profusion on semi-trailing stems. **SBP**

'Billy Green'
Raiser unknown–1966
The pale salmon-orange flowers are produced in terminal clusters, and in appearance are typical of *F. triphylla* hybrids though are possibly not of this origin. (*F. triphylla* hybrids, in general, are not described as being single or double because of the very distinctive shape of the flower – see page 86.) Upright growth. Has been used successfully by exhibitors **P**

'Billy Green' (see page 85)

'Bishops Bells'
Gadsby–Britain 1970. Semi-double
The tube and very long sepals are rose-red in colour. The corolla is bishop's violet, veined in red, and the large flowers are produced on strong, upright growth. **P**

'Blue Bush'
Gadsby–Britain 1973. Single
The flowers are small but freely produced. The sepals are red, and the corolla blue fading to violet. A good hardy plant. **H**

'Blue Pearl'
Martin–USA 1955. Double
The large flowers have a pink-coloured tube and sepals and a clear blue corolla. The blooms are very freely produced and come early. A good bush cultivar but will also make a nice hanging basket. The flower of 'Pinwheel' is very similar in appearance. **BP**

'Blue Petticoat'
Evans and Reeves–USA 1954. Double
This beautiful cultivar has a silvery lilac corolla which ages to a shade of pink. The tube and sepals are pink. The medium sized flowers are produced on thin, trailing stems. **B**

'Blue Waves'
Waltz–USA 1954. Double
The tube and sepals are scarlet. The large flowers have a deep violet-blue corolla streaked with rose. Upright, bushy growth. **SP**

'Blush o' Dawn'
Martin–USA 1962. Double
The tube and sepals are waxy white, but the main attraction of this exceptional flower is the silvery grey-blue

'Blue Waves'

corolla. The blooms are medium to large in size and the growth is upright but lax. Like 'Countess of Maritza' and other cultivars with this coloration the growth is rather slow. **BP**

'Bobby Wingrove'
Wingrove–Britain 1966. Single
The small, mainly red flowers are borne on a spreading, upright plant. The blooms are produced in great profusion over a long period. **P**

'Bon Accorde'
Crousse–France 1861. Single
The flowers of this old cultivar stand out erect from the stiff, upright stems. The tube and sepals are a waxy white colour and the corolla is bluish-purple. A rather similar cultivar is 'Estelle Marie'. **P**

'Bonnie Lass'
Waltz–USA 1962. Double
The tube and sepals are pale pink and white; the corolla is a lilac colour which fades with age. The medium sized blooms are freely produced on upright stems. **P**

'Bountiful'
Munkner–USA 1963. Double
The tube is very pale pink and the similarly coloured sepals are tipped green. The corolla is exceptionally fully double and beautifully shaped, and is a milky white colour. The large flowers are freely produced on fairly upright growth. With a little extra attention it will make a good medium sized standard. **SP**

Far left: 'Bon Accorde'

Left: 'Bountiful'

'Bridesmaid'
Tiret–USA 1952. Double
The corolla is a pale lilac colour which deepens towards the petal margins. The tube and sepals are white, flushed with pink. The medium sized flowers are freely produced. The growth is upright and this cultivar has been much used by exhibitors. **P**

'Brodsworth'
Nuttall–Britain 1977. Single
The tube and sepals are cherry red, the corolla deep purple. The medium sized flowers are freely produced. Upright, vigorous and bushy growth. Hardy. **HP**

'Brookwood Joy'
Gilbert–Britain 1983. Double
The tube and sepals are white or faintly pink. The corolla is marbled with blue and pink. The flowers are large and produced freely on upright growth. A very clear coloration; this new cultivar would appear to have a promising future. **SP**

'Brutus'
Lemoine–France 1897. Single
The medium sized red and purple flowers are produced in profusion in the classic form. The foliage is dark green and the growth very strong and upright. Will grow well even under unsuitable conditions. **HP**

'Buttercup'
Paskesen–USA 1976. Single
This name is misleading, as it is the shape of the flower rather than its colour which gives this modern American hybrid its name. The tube and sepals are pale orange and the corolla is a deeper shade of the same colour. The flowers are medium sized and freely produced. Upright growth. **P**

'Caballero'
Kennett–USA 1965. Double
The corolla is large and of a bluish-purple colour streaked with salmon pink. Petaloids can vary from red to white. The tube and sepals are salmon-pink. A lax bush or trailer. **BP**

'Caesar'
Castro–USA 1967. Double
The flowers are enormous; the corolla is an unusual shade of plum purple, while the tube and sepals are red. This cultivar initially tries to grow upright, but the weight of the flowers ensures a trailing habit. **B**

'Candlelight'
Waltz–USA 1959. Double
The tube and sepals are gleaming white with a pink flush on the underside of the sepals. The corolla is rose at the base, changing to a very dark purple-lilac, and fading to a reddish colour with age. The flowers are large and freely produced on an upright, well branching plant. **SP**

'Cara Mia'
Schnabel–USA 1957. Semi-double
The long, pointed and reflexed sepals are pale pink and the corolla deep red. The flowers are medium sized but freely produced. Trailing growth. **B**

'Carmel Blue'
Hodges–USA 1956. Single
The long tube and curled sepals are a glistening white. The long corolla is a mid blue colour which fades with age. Exceptionally free flowering; the medium sized blooms are produced on an upright bushy plant. **SP**

'Carnival'
Tiret–USA 1956. Double
The tube and sepals are white tipped with green. The very long corolla is a

bright spiraea red colour. The flowers are large and come early in the season. A lax bush or trailer. **BP**

'Caroline'
Miller–Britain 1967. Single
The tube and sepals are cream, flushed pink. The large corolla is a beautiful pale cyclamen purple; the petals flare out and, in a mature flower, open flat. Upright growth. This cultivar has tremendous appeal and is always admired wherever shown. **P**

'Cascade'
Lagen–USA 1937. Single
The long tube and sepals are white, with an overlay of pink. The corolla is a deep cerise-pink colour. The flowers are produced in abundance on trailing stems. **B**

'Celadore'
Hall–Britain 1979. Double
This large flower is a deep orchid-pink colour. The growth is upright but trails when weighed down with the heavy blooms. New and good. **BP**

'Celia Smedley'
Roe–Britain 1970. Single
The main feature of this cultivar is its very strong upright growth and the bright currant-red colour of the corolla. The sepals and tube are pale pink. The medium sized flowers are very freely produced. **P**

'Checkerboard'
Walker and Jones–USA 1948. Single
A very dainty and distinctive flower. The red tube contrasts well with the white sepals and deep red corolla. Strong, upright growth. **SP**

'Cheviot Princess'
Ryle–Britain 1977. Single
The long sepals and short tube are white. The corolla is a clear, bright red colour. Excellent bushy, upright growth. This is an attractive new cultivar. **P**

'Chillerton Beauty'
Bass–Britain 1847. Single
The small flowers have pink sepals and a mauve-purple corolla. The blooms are freely produced on upright, arching stems. Very hardy. **HP**

'Citation'
Hodges–USA 1953. Single
Very pale pink sepals and tube. The pink-veined white corolla opens flat like a saucer. A very free-flowering cultivar; upright growth. Should not be allowed to get too cold in winter. 'Spotlight' and 'Impudence' are cultivars of similar appearance. **P**

'Cliff's Hardy'
Gadsby–Britain 1966. Single
The tube is red; and the sepals are red, tipped green. The corolla is a campanula-violet colour. A good hardy plant with freely produced medium sized flowers. **HP**

'Cliff's Unique'
Gadsby–Britain 1976. Double
The tube is short and pink in colour and the sepals are pink with green tips. The mid-blue corolla matures to a mauve pink; medium sized, well formed blooms. If the plant is grown 'hard' the flowers are held erect. Beautiful and different. Upright, very bushy growth. **SP**

'Cloth of Gold'
Stafford–Britain 1863. Single
This cultivar is grown for its golden-yellow leaves which have a reddish reverse. The red and purple flowers are not freely produced. Bushy but rather horizontal growth. **P**

'Cliff's Unique'
(see page 89)

'Cloverdale Jewel'
Gadsby–Britain 1974. Semi-double
The tube and sepals are deep pink and the corolla is a mid-blue colour. The medium sized flowers are produced in great quantity. The great beauty of this plant is its ability to be trained in any desired form with minimum effort by the grower. **SP**

'Cloverdale Pearl'
Gadsby–Britain 1974. Single
The tube and sepals are pale pink and white with a tinge of green. The medium sized corolla is pearly white. This hybrid is very free flowering, and like 'Cloverdale Jewel' easy to grow. 'Coconut Ice', a seedling from 'Iced Champagne' × 'Cloverdale Pearl' is similar in appearance. **SP**

'Coachman'

'Coachman'
Bright–Britain c. *1910. Single*
The tube and sepals are a very pale salmon-orange colour. The corolla is a rich orange with an overlay of red. The medium sized flowers are produced freely on a very lax bush of pendent growth. Similar in appearance to 'Claire de Lune'. **SBP**

'Constellation'
Schnabel–USA 1957. Double
There are two other fuchsias named 'Constellation' but neither can be confused with this superb cultivar, which has large, pure white blooms with a slight greenish tinge to the sepals. It is very free flowering and of good constitution and growth. **SP**

'Coquet Dale'
Ryle–Britain 1976. Double
Another new cultivar of great merit. The tube and sepals are pink and the well shaped corolla a lilac-blue colour. Medium to large sized blooms; upright, bushy growth. **SP**

'Corallina'
Pince–Britain 1844. Single
The tube and sepals are scarlet and the corolla purple. The medium sized flowers are freely produced and the foliage has a bronze tint. The growth is arching and spreading. Very hardy. **HP**

'Core'ngrato'
Blackwell–Britain 1964. Double
The long tube and the sepals are a pale pink colour. The corolla opens a shade of deep red and fades to an orange-red colour with salmon markings. The medium sized flowers are produced on vigorous, upright growth. **P**

'Corsair'
Kennett–USA 1965. Double
The tube and sepals are a waxy white, the very large corolla deep blue marbled with white. Best grown as a trailer because of the weight of the blooms. **B**

'Dark Eyes' (see page 92)

'Cotton Candy'
Tiret–USA 1962. Double
The flower is basically white but tinged with delicate pale pink. The medium sized, fluffy flowers are freely produced on an upright plant. **SP**

'Countess of Maritza'
Holmes–Britain 1977. Double
The tube and sepals are a very pale pink and the large corolla is a silvery grey-blue colour similar to 'Blush o' Dawn'. The form of growth is trailing or a lax bush. Rather slow in growth, like all cultivars with this coloration. **BP**

'Crackerjack'
Walker–USA 1961. Single or semi-double
The tube and sepals are white tinged with pink. The petals flare out and are a beautiful pale blue colour. The growth is strong but horizontal. **SBP**

'Curly Q'
Kennett–USA 1961. Single
The tube and sepals are light red. The sepals roll to form a circle and the corolla is a violet-purple colour. The small flowers are freely produced on a large. Lax growth **B**

'Dancing Flame'
Stubbs–USA 1981. Double
The tube and sepals are a pinkish-orange colour and the corolla is in shades of deep orange. The flower can vary in size from medium to very large. Lax growth. **B**

'Dark Eyes'
Erickson–USA 1958. Double
The tube and sepals are deep red. The corolla is a pure violet-blue colour. The petals are evenly rolled and help to form an impeccably shaped flower. The medium sized blooms are produced in profusion. This cultivar makes an exceptionally good standard despite being a little weak in early growth. **SP**

'Derby Imp'
Gadsby–Britain 1974. Single
The tube and sepals are crimson and the corolla is violet-blue in colour. An exceptionally free-flowering cultivar. The small blooms are produced on thin, multi-branched stems with small pointed leaves. Horizontal growth. **BP**

'Diana Wills'
Gadsby–Britain 1968. Double
The tube and green-tipped sepals are white. The large flowers have a bright red corolla with white streaks. Upright, bushy growth. **P**

'Display'
Smith–Britain 1881. Single
This outstanding cultivar can be trained with ease into any shape and will also make a good house plant. The growth is upright but with a slight tendency to weep when in full flower. The foliage is dense and dark green in colour. The medium sized, fluorescent pink flowers are abundantly produced. The petals flare out, forming a cone shape. This cultivar is hardy in all except the coldest areas and cannot be overpraised. **HBSP**

'Dollar Princess'
Lemoine–France 1912. Double
A very easily cultivated plant with medium sized red and purple flowers. Growth is upright and vigorous. Very hardy. **HSP**

'Dorothea Flower'
Thornley–Britain 1969. Single
The tube and sepals are white with a faint pink tinge. The corolla is violet-

blue with a pink flush at the base. Rather long flowers; upright bushy growth. Miss Flower, after whom this cultivar was named, founded the Dorking Fuchsia Society. **P**

'Drame'
Lemoine–France 1880. Semi-double
An old cultivar which is still commonly grown today. The strong stems arch gracefully and the leaves are a pale shade of green. The medium sized red and purple flowers are freely produced. Very hardy. This cultivar is similar to 'Charming'. **HSP**

'Dunrobin Bedder'
Melville–Britain 1890. Single
Very small red and purple flowers. Dwarf, spreading growth. Very hardy. **H**

'Dusky Rose'
Waltz–USA 1960. Double
A very large spreading flower in shades of dusky rose pink. Trailing growth. **BP**

'Eleanor Leytham'
Roe–Britain 1973. Single
The tube and sepals are white, flushed with pink. The pink petals are edged with deep pink. The small flowers are produced in profusion on strong, upright growth. **P**

'Elsa'
Origin unknown. Semi-double
The tube and sepals are pale pink and the corolla is a rosy purple colour. The flowers are medium to large in size. The growth is vigorous and bushy but can spread sideways. Similar to the cultivar 'Lena'. **SP**

'Emile de Wildeman'
see **'Fascination'**

'Empress of Prussia'
Hoppe–Britain 1868. Single
An outstanding hardy cultivar. The red and reddish-magenta flowers are medium to large in size and are produced in abundance. Upright, bushy growth. This hybrid is similar in appearance to 'Monsieur Thibaut'. **H**

'Enchanted'
Tiret–USA 1951. Double
The short tube and sepals are rosy red. The corolla is a reddish-purple colour overlaid with pink. Lax growth, best grown in a basket. **B**

'Eternal Flame'
Paskesen–USA 1971. Semi-double
The tube and sepals are a deep salmon-pink and the corolla is a dusky rose colour streaked with shades of orange. Medium sized flowers; upright, bushy growth. **P**

'Eva Boerg'
Yorke–Britain 1943. Single or semi-double
The tube and sepals are a very pale pink colour with green tinges. The medium sized flowers have a rosy purple coloured corolla with pink streaks. Lax bushy growth and a favourite for hanging baskets. This cultivar received an RHS Award of Merit in the 1962 hardiness trials. **HBPS**

'Evensong'
Colville–Britain 1967. Single
Upright, strong growth. The medium sized flowers are freely produced and are white with only a hint of pink at the base of the petals. **P**

'Fancy Pants'
Reedstrom–USA 1961. Double
The tube and sepals are red. The flowers are large and the purple corolla

fades to a reddish colour with age. The growth is in the form of a lax bush but this cultivar can easily be trained into other shapes. **SBP**

'Fascination'
Lemoine–France 1905. Double
This cultivar is correctly called 'Emile de Wildeman' but this name is now rarely used. The large flowers are a shade of deep pink and are very freely produced. The growth is upright and bushy. Easy to grow but can be temperamental with regard to feeding, and it requires more nitrogen than many other fuchsias. 'R.A.F.' is similar in appearance to this cultivar. **SP**

'Fiona'
Clark–Britain 1958. Single
The tube and sepals are white and the corolla is an attractive shade of blue; the medium sized flowers are long in appearance. The growth is strong and rather horizontal. **SBP**

'Flash'
Hazard–USA ?1930. Single
The small, bright red flowers are freely produced on strong, upright growth. This cultivar failed to receive an award in the RHS hardiness trials of 1975 to 1978 but is generally recognized as a good hardy plant. **HP**

'Flirtation Waltz'
Waltz–USA 1962. Double
A first class, medium sized flower in shades of pale pink. Strong, upright, bushy growth. The only fault to be found with this cultivar is that the stems are extremely brittle and need early support. **SP**

'Florentina'
Tiret–USA 1960. Double
The tube and sepals are clear white and the corolla is a deep wine red colour.

'Evensong' (see page 93)

Unusual colouring but the growth is rather weak and lax. **BP**

'Flying Cloud'
Reiter–USA 1949. Double
A large flower which is pure white when kept shaded. Rather spreading growth; one of the best double white cultivars. **BP**

'Forward Look'
Gadsby–Britain 1972. Single
The short tube and sepals are pink with green tinges. The medium sized corolla is a mid-blue colour fading to

'Flirtation Waltz'

'Garden News'

mauve. The flowers are held out horizontally; close jointed, bushy, upright growth. **P**

'Frosted Flame'
Handley Britain 1975. Single
The tube and sepals are white. The corolla is a bright flame colour with the colour deepening towards the edge of the petals. Large, barrel shaped, freely produced blooms; trailing growth. **B**

'Garden News'
Handley–Britain 1978. Double
The tube and sepals are pink. The corolla is a bright magenta red. The large flowers are produced on strong, upright stems. This cultivar not only makes a superb pot plant but is also hardy. **HSP**

'Gartenmeister Bonstedt'
Bonstedt–Germany 1905. Single
One of the *F. triphylla* group of hybrids with characteristically long flowers produced in terminal clusters.

'Hawkshead' (see page 97)

The flowers are brick red in colour and are produced on a plant with deep green leaves with a bronze hue. Cultivars of this type need a minimum winter temperature of 10°C (50°F) but they will bed out very well in summer. None of the *F. triphylla* hybrids is easy to train into standards. **P**

'Gay Fandango'
Nelson–USA 1951. Double
The tube and sepals are pink. The rose-coloured corolla is formed in tiers, making the flower appear long. Medium to large blooms borne on horizontal growth. **SBP**

'Genii' see **'Jeane'**

'Gilda'
Handley–Britain 1971. Double
The short tube and broad sepals are salmon pink. The corolla is rose red. The flowers are large and very freely produced. The red stems are upright and bear yellowish-green leaves with red veins. **P**

'Golden Dawn'
Haag–USA 1951. Single
The corolla is a light orange colour overlaid with pink. The tube and sepals are a pale salmon-orange colour. Medium sized flowers; upright growth. A little extra work will be needed to make a good standard. **SP**

'Golden Lena'
Origin unknown. Semi-double
The tube and sepals are pale pink. The corolla is a shade of magenta; medium sized flowers. The foliage is variegated green and yellow. Like most cultivars with variegated foliage it is susceptible to botrytis of the stem when young. Very lax, bushy growth. A sport from 'Lena'. **HBP**

'Golden Marinka'
Weber–USA 1955. Single
Beautiful deep red, medium sized flowers. The foliage is splendidly variegated in green and gold. Extremely attractive, but needs a little extra warmth in winter. Bushy, stiff growing, horizontal growth. This cultivar is mainly used in hanging baskets but it will make a reasonable standard. **SBP**

'Granada'
Schnabel–USA 1957. Double
A very large, classic red and purple flower. This is one of the best plants of this coloration. Large, dark green leaves. Upright bushy growth. **P**

'Hampshire Blue'
Clark–Britain 1983. Single
The tube and sepals are white and the long corolla is a very appealing shade of pale sky blue. The flowers are extremely profuse and are borne on upright stems. A sport from 'Carmel Blue'. **SP**

'Hampshire Prince'
Clark–Britain 1983. Double
The tube and sepals are pink. The very full corolla is a silvery lavender fading to pink. Very free flowering and early for a double. Upright growth. A sport from 'Prince of Peace'. **P**

'Hampshire Treasure'
Clark–Britain 1983. Double
The tube and sepals are a pale salmon orange. The corolla is multicoloured with shades of magenta, red, orange and yellowish orange. The flowers are very freely produced over a long period. Very good for summer bedding. A 'Bicentennial' × 'Lord Lonsdale' seedling. Horizontal, bushy growth, but will train to almost any shape. **SBP**

'Harry Gray'
Dunnett–Britain 1980. Double
A medium sized white flower, sometimes slightly tinged with pink. A very bushy but wiry form of growth with small leaves. A new fuchsia of outstanding quality; could be one of the best basket subjects of all time. **SBP**

'Hawkshead'
Travis–Britain 1962. Single
Small greenish-white flowers reminiscent of, but an improvement on, its parent, *F. magellanica* var. *molinae*. Very strong, upright growth. Very hardy. **HP**

'Heidi Ann'
Smith–Britain 1969. Double
The tube and sepals are cerise and the corolla is a lilac colour veined with cerise. Medium sized flowers. Compact, bushy, upright growth. Superb as a small pot plant. Suits commercial growers and exhibitors well. **SP**

'Heidi Weiss'
Tacolneston Nurseries–Britain 1973. Double
This is a sport from 'Heidi Ann' and retains all its progenitor's good qualities but differs in having a white corolla with scarlet veins. This is probably the same plant as 'White Ann'. **SP**

'Hi Jinks'
Kennett–USA 1968. Double
The tube is pink and the sepals are white with pink undersides. The large corolla is a purple colour with white streaks. Lax bush or trailing growth. **B**

'Howletts Hardy'
Howlett–Britain 1952. Single
The tube and sepals are scarlet and the corolla is a deep mauve colour with red veining. Upright, bushy growth. The bell-shaped flowers are medium sized and good for a hardy cultivar. **HP**

'Iced Champagne'
Jennings–Britain 1968. Single
The flowers are in two shades of pink. The medium sized blooms are produced in profusion on a compact, short jointed bush. **P**

'Igloo Maid'
Holmes–Britain 1972. Double
The large, double white flowers are tinged pink when the plant is grown in sunshine. The foliage is a delightful shade of greenish lemon-yellow. 'Annabel' has similar flowers (see page 84) The growth is strong and initially upright but it tends to spread with age. Can be grown as a pot plant but in the long term is probably best in a hanging basket. Makes a very good weeping standard. **SBP**

'Impudence'
Schnabel–USA 1957. Single
The tube and sepals are a deep pink colour. The white corolla opens flat like a saucer; upright growth. Very similar to 'Citation', but slightly easier to grow. **P**

'Indian Maid'
Waltz–USA 1962. Double
The tube and long sepals are scarlet. The corolla is a rich shade of royal purple. The deep green foliage and the richness of the flower colour gives this plant a handsome appearance. Trailing growth. **BP**

'Isle of Mull'
Tolley–Britain 1978. Single
The tube is light red in colour and the sepals a noticeably paler shade of the same colour. The corolla is a glowing

'Iced Champagne'

rosy magenta. The growth is upright and exceptionally bushy and short jointed. A superb cultivar. **SP**

'Jack Acland'
Haag–USA 1952. Single
The tube and sepals are pink and the long corolla is a bright rose colour. The flowers are produced in great abundance. It is a fairly upright grower but will make a good display in a hanging basket. This cultivar is similar in appearance to 'Jack Shahan'. **SBP**

'Jack Shahan'

'Jack Shahan'
Tiret–USA 1948. Single
This hybrid has similar flowers to 'Jack Acland' but is more lax in growth; it makes a good weeping standard. **SB**

'Jeane'
Reiter–USA 1951. Single
This cultivar is most frequently found under the name 'Genii' or 'Genie'. All these names would appear to have occurred by phonetic misspelling of the original name. The tube and sepals are red and the corolla a violet colour. The small flowers are produced among light yellowish-green foliage. The growth is upright and bushy. Very hardy. **HSP**

'Jennie Rachael'
Cheetham–Britain 1979. Double
The tube and sepals are tinged with pink. The full corolla is veined in shades of rose red, but one petal will often have a white patch. Very large flowers and leaves. **BP**

'Joy Patmore'
Turner–Britain 1961. Single
The tube and sepals are waxy white. The corolla flares wide open and is an unusually clear shade of bluish-purple. Very free flowering; upright growth. This cultivar is very similar in appearance to 'Lye's Excelsior'. **SP**

'Kegworth Beauty'
Smith–Britain 1974. Single
The long tube and sepals are a waxy white colour and the corolla is a shade of amaranth rose. The small flowers are produced over a very long period. Bushy, upright, short jointed growth. **P**

'Kernan Robson'
Tiret–USA 1958. Double
The tube and sepals are red and the

'Joy Patmore'

corolla is a smoky-red colour. Upright, bushy growth and large flowers. **SP**

'Kiwi'
Tiret–USA 1966. Double
The tube and sepals are pure white. The corolla is a plum purple colour with pink tinges. Large flowers. Early growth is upright, but will trail with age. **BP**

'Kolding Perle'
Origin unknown. Single
The tube and sepals are white, the corolla a cerise colour. Free flowering on upright growth. This cultivar possibly originated in Denmark, and is similar in appearance to 'Amy Lye'. **P**

'Kon-Tiki'
Tiret–USA 1965. Double
The tube and sepals are white and the full corolla is a shade of purplish blue with white petaloids. Distinctive coloration, large flowers. The growth is reasonably upright, but will trail under some conditions. **BP**

'La Campanella'
Blackwell–Britain 1968. Single or semi-double
The tube and sepals are white and the corolla is a bright purple-blue colour. The flowers are small but exceptionally profuse. The form of growth is a low wiry bush, dense and short jointed, but it is most commonly grown in a basket. Very fine. A similar cultivar but with more pendulous growth is 'Auntie Jinks'. **SBP**

'La Fiesta'
Kennett–USA 1962. Double
The tube and sepals are white. The very colourful corolla is a dianthus purple colour irregularly streaked with white. The growth is trailing and can sometimes be a little difficult to manage. **B**

'Lady Isobel Barnett'
Gadsby–Britain 1968. Single
The tube and sepals are light red and the corolla is a pale shade of rose-purple. This must be one of the most free flowering fuchsias yet produced. The growth is fairly strong and upright and the flowers are held out horizontally from the plant. Very fine and distinct. **P**

'Lady Kathleen Spence'

'Lady Kathleen Spence'
Ryle–Britain 1974. Single
The tube and sepals are pale pink. The corolla is a shade of pale lavender. The medium sized flowers are produced on a bushy, upright plant. **SP**

'Lady Thumb'
Roe–Britain 1966. Semi-double
The tube and sepals are light red and the corolla white with red veining. The growth is dwarf and very bushy. The small flowers are produced in profusion. Excellent for small pots, rockeries or as an edging plant in the garden. Very hardy. A sport from 'Tom Thumb'. **HP**

'Lakeside'
Thornley–Britain 1967. Single
The tube and sepals are red. The medium sized blooms have a bluish-violet corolla. Free branching, trailing growth. Popular with exhibitors for the hanging basket classes. **SB**

'La Neige'
Tiret–USA 1965. Double
The medium sized flowers are a creamy white colour with only a hint of pink. Vigorous, spreading growth. **BP**

'Laurie'
Antonelli–USA 1963. Double
The flowers are a shade of dusky pink and the sepals have greenish tips. The medium to large sized blooms are produced on strong, trailing stems. Deep green foliage. **SB**

'Lena'
Bunney–Britain 1862. Semi-double
The corolla is a rosy magenta shade and the sepals and tube are a pale pink colour. Medium sized flowers; lax growth. Very popular and hardy. **HSBP**

'Lena Dalton'
Reimers–USA 1953. Double
The tube and sepals are a pale pink colour. The corolla is clear blue, fading to mauve blue. Medium sized flowers; upright, bushy growth. **P**

'Leonora'
Tiret–USA 1960. Single
This plant produces medium sized, pure pink, bell shaped flowers. The growth is upright and bushy. A superb cultivar which is easy to grow to exhibition standard. **SP**

'Lindisfarne'
Ryle–Britain 1974. Semi-double
The very short tube and sepals are pale pink and the corolla is a rich violet-blue colour which resists fading. The flowers are only medium sized but they are produced in great profusion. The growth is upright, bushy, and short jointed. **P**

'Lord Lonsdale'
Raiser unknown. Single
The beautiful medium sized flowers are in shades of clear tangerine orange. Like the very similar cultivar 'Aurora Superba', it has characteristically curled and crinkled foliage which to the uninitiated may be thought to be caused by disease. This curling of the leaves is at its worst in winter and when the plants start to grow rapidly in the spring. This cultivar is worth growing for its colour alone. **P**

'Lye's Unique'
Lye–Britain 1886. Single
The tube and sepals are a waxy white colour and the corolla is salmon-orange. The medium sized flowers are produced on very strong, upright growth. **SP**

'Madame Cornelissen'
Cornelissen–Belgium 1860. Semi-double
The tube and sepals are scarlet and the corolla is white with scarlet veining. Small flowers, strong upright growth, dark green leaves. Hardy. **HSP**

'Mantilla'
Reiter–USA 1948
The long red tubular flowers produced are typical of the *F. triphylla* hybrids (see 'Gartenmeister Bonstedt'). The growth of this cultivar is unusual, as not many of this group have trailing stems, but see also' 'Trumpeter'. **B**

'Margaret'
Wood–Britain 1937. Semi-double
The medium sized flowers have a scarlet tube and sepals and a violet-coloured corolla with cerise veining. Upright, bushy growth. **HP**

'Margaret Brown'
Wood–Britain 1949. Single
The tube and sepals are light red and the corolla is a magenta colour. The smallish flowers are produced among light green foliage. The growth is upright and bushy. Very hardy. **HP**

'Marin Glow'
Reedstrom–USA 1954. Single
The tube and sepals are a pure waxy white, and the corolla is a glowing royal-purple colour which matures to a shade of magenta. The medium sized flowers are produced in profusion. The growth is strong, upright and bushy and this outstanding cultivar is very suitable for exhibition. **SP**

'Marinka'
Rozain-Boucharlat–France 1902. Single
The medium sized flowers are a shade of dark cherry red and the vigorous trailing stems are clothed with dark green leaves. This is the trailer by which all others are judged. It needs to be sited carefully for general display because of its overall dark appearance. **SB**

'Mary'
Bonstedt–Germany 1894
The scarlet flowers are up to 8 cm (3 in) long and the foliage is a sage green colour; upright growth. An *F. triphylla* hybrid (see 'Gartenmeister Bonstedt'). **P**

'Melody'
Reiter–USA 1942. Single
The tube and sepals are a pale rose pink and the corolla is a cyclamen purple colour. Medium sized flowers; bright green foliage on upright, bushy growth. Very easy to grow to a good standard. **SP**

'Merry England'
Gadsby–Britain 1968. Double
The tube is red and the sepals are white with pink undersides. The corolla is a deep violet blue flushed with orchid pink. The flowers are large and are produced on upright, bushy stems. **P**

'Merry Mary'
Castro–USA 1965. Double
The tube and sepals are pink. The corolla is white, with pink at the base of the petals and pink veining. The showy flowers are large; trailing growth. **B**

'Midnight Sun'
Waltz–USA 1960. Double
The tube and broad sepals are pink. The corolla has a deep reddish-purple colour. The shorter outer petals have salmon-pink at their base. The flowers are large, and growth is upright and vigorous. **P**

'Mission Bells'

'Mieke Meursing'
Hopwood–Britain 1968. Single or semi-double
The medium to small flowers have red sepals and a pink corolla. The plant produces masses of flowers on an extremely compact and bushy plant. An ideal exhibitor's cultivar, but not very popular with the general public. **P**

Opposite: 'Lady Thumb' (see page 100)

Below: 'Morning Light'

'Miss California'
Hodges–USA 1950. Semi-double
The tube and sepals are pink, the corolla white with a hint of pink, and the medium sized flowers are very elegant and freely produced. The plant is rather slow to grow in the early stages, but is very rewarding in the long term. Upright, easily trained growth. **SP**

'Mission Bells'
Walker and Jones–USA 1948. Single
The tube and sepals are scarlet and the corolla is an intense, rich purple colour. The medium sized flowers are distinctive and shaped like a bell. Stiff, upright growth. **P**

'Miss Vallejo'
Tiret–USA 1958. Double
The flower is in two shades of pink; the tube and sepals are paler and are tinged with green. The large flowers are globular in shape. Requires warmth in winter; a lax bush or trailing form. **BP**

'Monsieur Thibaut'
Lemoine–France 1898. Single
The medium sized flowers are red and magenta and are produced on extremely strong, upright stems. Very hardy. This cultivar is similar to 'Empress of Prussia'. **HP**

'Morning Light'
Waltz–USA 1960. Double
The tube is pink and the sepals are pink at the base turning white with green tips. The fully double corolla is a beautiful combination of lavender and pink. The foliage is a pale yellowish-green colour. Very attractive. Bushy, fairly upright growth. **SP**

'Mountain Mist'
Crockett–Britain 1971. Double
The tube is white, and the sepals are white tipped with pink. The corolla is a pastel shade of silvery lavender. Large flowers; upright growth. **P**

'Mr A. Huggett'
Origin unknown. Single
The corolla is a mauve-pink colour with magenta edged petals and the tube and sepals are red. The flowers are small, but they are profuse and are produced over a long period. Upright, bushy growth. Suitable for exhibition. Hardy in sheltered areas. **P**

'Mrs Lovell Swisher'
Evans and Reeves–USA 1942. Single
The long tube and sepals are pale pink, the corolla a rose-red colour. The flowers are small and dainty and are produced on upright stems. **SP**

'Mrs Popple'
Elliot–Britain 1899. Single
The medium sized flowers are red and purple-violet. The growth is upright and bushy. This cultivar is very hardy and suitable for hedging purposes. **HP**

'Mrs W. Rundle'
Rundle–Britain 1883. Single
The very long tube and sepals are pale pink, and the corolla is a bright orange-red colour. The medium sized flowers are freely produced on a lax bush. Very graceful. **SBP**

'Nancy Lou'
Stubbs–USA 1971. Double
The tube and sepals are a pale pink colour and the corolla is a clear white. Large, beautifully shaped flowers. Upright growth. **P**

'Nellie Nuttall'
Roe–Britain 1977. Single
There have been several cultivars which the raisers have claimed to be better than 'Snowcap'. This is possibly the only one which actually is an improvement. The medium sized flowers are incredibly abundant and tend to point upwards (unlike 'Snowcap'). The growth is short jointed and bushy. Outstanding for general display and exhibition. The author has not tried this cultivar as a standard but it should prove suitable. **SP**

'Northumbrian Belle'
Ryle–Britain 1973. Single
The tube and sepals are deep pink; the corolla is long and a clear, deep sky-blue colour. The medium sized flowers are produced on strong, free-branching stems which generally carry the mass of flowers without the need for much support. **SP**

'Orange Crush'
Handley–Britain 1972. Single
The tube and sepals are a salmon-orange colour, while the corolla is a deep shade of orange. The medium sized flowers are freely produced on vigorous, upright stems. **P**

'Orange Crystal'
Handley–Britain 1980. Single
The tube is light orange and the sepals are similarly coloured and tipped with green. The corolla is a clear, bright orange colour. The flowers are medium sized and the growth is upright, bushy and compact. **P**

'Orange Drops'
Martin–USA 1963. Single
The tube and sepals are pale orange and the corolla a deep orange colour. The medium sized flowers are produced in profusion on stems which tend to grow sideways. This cultivar will make a low bush or a hanging basket. **BP**

'Orange Flare'
Handley–Britain 1972. Single
The short thick tube and short sepals are salmon-orange and the corolla is coloured in shades of light and dark orange. Medium sized flowers; growth is upright and bushy. **P**

'Orange Mirage'
Tiret–USA 1970. Single
The corolla is rather long in shape and an unusual deep smoky-orange colour. The tube and sepals are salmon-orange. The very strong growth is distinctly horizontal in habit and this cultivar is excellent in a large hanging basket or as a weeping standard. **SBP**

'Oriental Sunrise'
Soo Yun–USA 1975. Single
The medium sized flowers are in shades of light and dark orange. The stems are red and semi-trailing in habit. **BP**

'Other Fellow'
Hazard–USA 1946. Single
The tube is waxy white and the sepals are white tipped with green. The corolla is a light pink colour, paler at the base. Small, freely produced flowers. A very beautiful cultivar; upright, bushy growth. **P**

'Pacquesa'
Clyne–Britain 1974. Single
A cultivar with this form and colour will always be compared with 'Ballet Girl', and this modern hybrid wins handsomely. Not only are the red and white flowers produced more freely but the plant is better natured, stronger and more bushy. The flowers are similar in size to 'Ballet Girl' but the colour is brighter and more glowing. **SP**

'Peppermint Stick'
Walker and Jones–USA 1950. Double
The tube and sepals are red. The corolla is bicoloured, the centre petals being royal purple and the outer petals pale rose with streaks of royal purple. Medium to large flowers; upright, bushy growth. **SP**

'Phenomenal'
Lemoine–France 1869. Double
The very large flowers have a rich red coloured tube and sepals, and a deep indigo-blue corolla. The growth is upright and bushy. This cultivar was Highly Commended in the RHS hardiness trial 1965, and as such must be one of the largest flowered hardy fuchsias available. **HSP**

'Phyllis'
Brown–Britain 1938. Semi-double
The medium sized, rose pink flowers are freely produced. The growth is strong and upright. Very suitable for fuchsia hedges. **HSP**

'Pink Darling'
Machado–USA 1961. Single
The tube and sepals are two shades of pink; the corolla is a pinkish shade of lavender. The small flowers are held semi-erect from the bushy, upright growth. Very rewarding to grow and with frequent pinching this cultivar will make an excellent show plant. **P**

'Pink Galore'
Walker–USA 1958. Double
The flower is large and a beautiful shade of candy pink. The growth is trailing, with deep green, glossy leaves. This cultivar's only fault, along with many other trailers, is that the flowers tend to appear mainly on the ends of the long stems, leaving the rest of the plant relatively bare. **B**

'Pacquesa' (see page 105)

'Pink Marshmallow'
Stubbs–USA 1971. Double
This cultivar freely produces enormous blooms. The flowers are white with the faintest hint of pink. The trailing growth is vigorous and fairly bushy. Very large flowered fuchsias can often be disappointing to grow, but this one is remarkably good. **B**

'Pixie'
Russell–Britain 1960. Single
The tube and sepals are light red in colour and the corolla is mauve with red veins. The medium sized blooms are produced on vigorous, upright stems clothed with pale green leaves. Highly Commended in the RHS hardiness trials 1978. **HSP**

'Plenty'
Gadsby–Britain 1974. Single
This cultivar is well named as it produces plenty of medium sized flowers. The tube and sepals are red and the corolla is violet-purple. The compact growth is upright and bushy. Very suitable for exhibition. **SP**

'Prelude'
Blackwell–Britain 1957. Single
The medium sized flowers are produced in clusters. The tube and sepals are red and the corolla is a magenta colour. Upright growth. It has received the RHS Award of Merit for hardiness. **HP**

'Prelude'
Kennett–USA 1958. Double
The second fuchsia with this name. This is an unusual hybrid with a pinkish tube and sepals and a multi-coloured corolla in shades of royal purple, pink and white. The growth is trailing, with rather short stems. **BP**

'President Margaret Slater'
Taylor–Britain 1972. Single
The long tube and sepals are creamy white; the corolla is a beautiful shade of pinkish plum. The stiff but trailing growth is dense and very well branched. The habit and colour of this cultivar is superb but it flowers rather late in the season, especially for a single, and for this reason alone will not be used by commercial growers. **SB**

'Preston Guild'
Thornley–Britain 1971. Single
The flowers are small but brightly coloured. The tube and sepals are pure white and the corolla a bright sky-blue colour which fades to mauve. The plant grows strongly and the stems are stiff and upright. **P**

'Prince of Peace'
Davis–USA 1970. Double
The tube and sepals are pale pink. The corolla is an unusual reddish-plum colour which ages to a lustrous rose. The flowers are very large and the vigorous, upright growth will trail under the weight of the blooms. **P**

'Prosperity'
Gadsby–Britain 1970. Double
The tube and sepals are crimson and the corolla is a pale pink colour. The medium sized flowers are well shaped and borne freely on strong, upright and bushy growth. Hardy. **HSP**

'R.A.F.'
Garson–USA 1942. Double
The large flowers have a red tube and sepals and a dusky, pink-coloured corolla veined with cerise. The growth is lax but upright. This cultivar is similar to 'Fascination' but less temperamental. **SP**

'Pink Marshmallow'

'R.A.F.'

'Ruth King' (see page 108)

'Raspberry'
Tiret–USA 1959. Double
The tube and sepals are pale pink and the corolla is an unusual shade of deep pink. The growth is upright with large, mid-green leaves. **P**

'Red Spider'
Reiter–USA 1946. Single
The long tube and narrow recurving sepals are deep red and the corolla is a deep, dusky red colour. The flowers are produced very freely on vigorous, trailing growth. A rather poor choice of name for a good fuchsia. **B**

'Riccartonii'
Young–Scotland c. 1830. Single
The hardiest *F. magellanica* hybrid. The red and purple flowers are very striking; this is one of the most widely used fuchsias for hedging. **HP**

'Rose of Castile'
Banks–Britain 1855. Single
The tube and sepals are white and the corolla is a light purple colour, whitish at the base of the petals. The small to medium sized flowers are produced in profusion. Upright, bushy growth. A particularly bright and cheerful hardy cultivar. 'Rose of Castile Improved' is very similar but has larger flowers and a more vigorous habit. **HSP**

'Rough Silk'
Baker–Britain 1970. Single
The tube and long sepals are very pale pink and the long corolla is an unusual shade of deep red. The vigorous, trailing stems are clothed with dark green leaves. A very beautiful cultivar, which deserves to be more widely grown. **SB**

'Royal Velvet'
Waltz–USA 1962. Double
A real beauty. The large flowers, with a red tube and sepals, have a luminous purple corolla and are very freely produced. The leaves are dark green and the stems are strong, upright and free branching. This cultivar makes a magnificent standard and is exceptionally easy to train; only when it has been grown for some years are all its good qualities fully appreciated. **SP**

'Rufus'
Nelson–USA 1952. Single
The medium sized, mid-red flowers are produced on extremely strong, upright stems. This cultivar is easy to grow and can make an enormous standard after only one year's growth. Sometimes called 'Rufus the Red'. **SP**

'Ruth King'
Tiret–USA 1967. Double
The sepals and tube are deep pink in colour and the corolla is dusky lilac and pale pink. An unusual and interesting coloration; medium to large sized flowers. **SPB**

'Sally Ann'
Pennisi–USA 1971. Double
The tube and sepals are white and the corolla is coloured with several shades of pink. Large flowers; trailing growth. **B**

'Salmon Glow'
Handley–Britain 1978. Single
The long tube and short sepals are pale to mid-salmon orange. The corolla is a shade of deep salmon orange. Medium sized flowers and light green leaves; lax bush type growth. **BP**

'Satellite'
Kennett–USA 1965. Single
The tube and sepals are white and the corolla is a deep, wine red colour with irregular streaks of white. Large

flowers; upright growth. Very attractive. **P**

'Sea Shell'
Evans–USA 1954. Double
The tube and reflexing sepals are a very pale pink colour. The corolla is pale pink with deep pink veins. Upright, bushy growth. **P**

'Shady Blue'
Gadsby–Britain 1970. Single
The short tube and broad sepals are red. The corolla is a violet-blue colour which changes to almost pink at the base of the petals. Large flowers, upright growth. **P**

'Shooting Star'
Martin–USA 1965. Semi-double
The tube and sepals are light red in colour; the corolla has a purple centre with purple and red outer petals. This coloration gives the medium sized flowers a striking appearance. The habit is of a lax bush or trailing form. There is another fuchsia with this name, raised by Baker in 1970, but it should not be confused with 'Shooting Star' (Martin) as it has a fully double flower. **BP**

'Sleigh Bells'
Schnabel–USA 1954. Single
The white sepals reflex and touch the tube. The medium sized flowers are pure white with a bell shaped corolla. The growth is upright and reasonably bushy. **SP**

'Snowcap'
Henderson–Britain c. *1880. Semi-double*
A deservedly well known cultivar. The red and white flowers are not large but they are freely produced. The plant's habit is upright and bushy and it can be used for training into almost any form except a hanging basket. The only cultivar that really challenges the supremacy of 'Snowcap' is 'Nellie Nuttall', and although better in many ways it does not have the vigour of 'Snowcap', which is hardy in many areas. Similar cultivars are 'Ice Cap' and 'Madame van der Strasse'.**SP**

'Son of Thumb'
Gubler–Britain 1978. Single
This is a sport of 'Tom Thumb' with a mauve-lilac corolla. The other good qualities of its progenitor are retained. **HP**

'Sonata'
Tiret–USA 1960. Double
The tube and sepals are pale pink in colour and the corolla is a shade of creamy white. This is a large flowered cultivar, and for its size the blooms are early and freely produced. It needs a little extra warmth in winter and will make a good bush if kept well pinched. **BP**

'Sophisticated Lady'
Martin–USA 1964. Double
The very long sepals and the tube are pale pink; the corolla is a creamy white colour. The flowers are large and the growth is trailing. The blooms are rather similar in appearance to 'Angel's Flight'. **B**

'Southgate'
Walker and Jones–USA 1951. Double
The large blooms are nearly one shade of soft pink, but the sepals have greenish tips. The growth is moderately vigorous and upright and the foliage is a dark, glossy green colour. This cultivar is easy to grow as a standard. **SP**

'Spion Kop'
Jones–Britain 1973. Double
The tube and sepals are pale pink, and the corolla white veined in red. The

'Southgate' (see page 109)

medium sized flowers are profuse and the habit of growth is upright and bushy. The merits of this cultivar are often considerably underestimated, and it should be included in every collection. It will make a superb standard. **SP**

'Stanley Cash'
Pennisi–USA 1970. Double
The short tube and sepals are a waxy white colour. The full corolla is a very deep, sky blue colour verging on royal purple. The flowers are very large and freely produced on trailing stems. The blooms are almost identical to 'Capri' but the habit is a great improvement on this slightly older cultivar. **SB**

'Strawberry Delight'
Gadsby–Britain 1969. Double
The tube and sepals are red in colour and the corolla is white, heavily flushed with pink and veined in red. The medium to large sized flowers are produced on strong, arching stems. The foliage is a yellowish-green colour with a pronounced bronze cast. **BP**

Opposite: 'Thornley's Hardy' (see page 113)

Right: 'Stanley Cash'

'Strawberry Sundae'
Kennett–USA 1958. Double
The tube and broad sepals are white. The corolla is lilac and pink, fading to an all pink coloration. Large flowers; very vigorous, trailing growth. **B**

'Sunray'
Rudd–Britain 1872. Single
The flowers, which are small, red and purple in colour, are relatively insignificant. This cultivar is grown for its foliage, which is silvery green and cream and shaded with red. The growth is bushy and rather upright, but 'Sunray' can also be used in a hanging basket. **BP**

'Susan Ford'
Clyne–Britain 1972. Double
The short tube and reflexing sepals are a bright rose colour. The corolla is imperial purple, fading with age. The medium sized flowers are freely produced. Upright, bushy growth. **P**

'Susan Travis'
Travis–Britain 1958. Single
The medium sized flowers are pink. Vigorous growth forming a nicely rounded bush. Highly Commended in the RHS hardiness trials 1978. **HP**

'Swanley Gem'
Cannell–Britain 1901. Single
The tube and sepals are a rich red and the corolla is a violet colour, lightening towards the base. The petals flare out, forming a circle. Upright, bushy growth. **P**

'Sweet Leilani'
Tiret–USA 1957. Double
The tube and sepals are a light red colour and the corolla is a shade of smoky blue. The flowers are large, but are unfortunately produced very late in the season. Strong, bushy growth. **BP**

'Swingtime'
Tiret–USA 1950. Double
The short tube and sepals are one shade of bright red. The beautifully formed corolla is a milky white colour with faint red veining. The flowers are large, and for their size produced in incredible quantity. The growth is vigorous, bushy and upright but arches or trails under the weight of the blooms. 'Pathetique' is another cultivar similar to 'Swingtime', and although it produces smaller blooms on wiry stems so is 'Molesworth'. In a list of the best six fuchsias 'Swingtime', along with 'Display' and 'Snowcap', would be on most growers' lists. **SBP**

'Symphony'
Niederholzer–USA 1944. Single
The tube and sepals are pink. The corolla is a deep violet-blue colour fading with age. The beautifully shaped, medium sized flowers are produced on tall, upright stems. **SP**

'Tennessee Waltz'
Walker and Jones–USA 1951. Double
The tube and reflexed sepals are red, and the corolla is a shade of lavender with pink markings. The flower size is medium to large and the growth habit is strong, bushy and upright. This cultivar was awarded the RHS Highly Commended Certificate for hardiness, although for best results it will need a sheltered position in the garden. 'Tennessee Waltz' will also make an easy-to-grow standard. **HSP**

'Texas Longhorn'
Walker–USA 1960. Semi-double or double
The tube and very long sepals are red and the corolla is white, veined with red. Because the long sepals are held out horizontally, the blooms can measure up to 23 cm (9 in) across on a well grown plant. The growth is upright, but willowy and difficult to train though it will make a reasonable standard. This cultivar needs warmth in winter and is either liked or intensely despised. **SP**

'Thalia'
Attributed to Turner–Britain 1855.
The long, orange-scarlet flowers are borne in terminal clusters in the usual fashion for *F. triphylla* hybrids. The deep bronze-green foliage is red on the underside. Vigorous, upright growth. Very beautiful but similar to 'Gartenmeister Bonstedt'. There are doubts that the cultivar grown today is Turner's 'Thalia' as the above differs considerably from his original description. **P**

'The Doctor'
Origin unknown. Single
The long tube and sepals are salmon-pink and the corolla is a deep reddish-orange colour. The flowers are medium to large in size and very freely produced. The growth is strong and it tends to grow outwards horizontally. This cultivar can be grown as a bush but it is better as an easily grown

weeping standard or in a hanging basket. **SB**

'The Marvel'
Vicarage Farm Nurseries–Britain 1968. Single
The tube and the green-tipped sepals are white and the corolla is a pinkish-lavender colour. The flowers are large and the growth is upright. **P**

'Thornley's Hardy'
Thornley–Britain 1970. Single
The tube and sepals are white and the corolla is a red colour. The flowers are small but the overall appearance of the plant is one of great beauty. The nature of the growth is low and spreading. This cultivar was tested for hardiness by the RHS, but received no award. It is still worth trying in the garden because of its elegant appearance. **HSP**

'Ting-a-Ling'
Schnabel–USA 1959. Single
The medium to large white flowers are freely produced. The petals flare out in a saucer shape and the growth is stiff and uncompromisingly upright. Like all the white-flowered cultivars it is rather susceptible to botrytis. **P**

'Tom Thumb'
Baudinat–France 1850. Single
The tube and sepals are red and the corolla is a purple colour. The small blooms are produced in vast numbers on a compact, very bushy plant. This cultivar received the RHS First Class Certificate for hardiness in 1962. **HP**

'Trail Blazer'
Reiter–USA 1951. Double
The tube and sepals are red and the corolla is a deep red colour. The large, rather long flowers are freely produced on cascading stems. Vigorous growth. **B**

'Trase'
Dawson–Britain 1959. Double or semi-double
The medium sized flowers have a cerise-coloured tube and sepals, and a white corolla heavily flushed with deep pink. The growth is upright, bushy and hardy. **HP**

'Traudchen Bonstedt'
Bonstedt–Germany 1905.
Another member of the *F. triphylla* group. The long flowers are a pale creamy pink colour throughout, and the leaves are pale green flushed with bronze and red on the underside. **P**

'Treasure'
Niederholzer–USA 1946. Double
The tube and sepals are pale pink and the full corolla is a pale silvery violet-pink. The large flowers are freely produced on the upright, bushy stems. **P**

'Tricolorii' ('Tricolor')
Potney–Britain, date unknown. Single
This cultivar is correctly called *F. magellanica* var. *macrostemma* 'Versicolor' but is usually listed by nurserymen as 'Tricolorii' or 'Tricolor'. The small flowers are red and purple. The cream and silvery green foliage is heavily suffused with red. The growth is upright and bushy, and it is very hardy. **HP**

'Trudy'
Gadsby–Britain 1969. Single
The tube and sepals are red and the corolla is a cyclamen-purple colour. The small flowers are similar to, but an improvement on, 'Chillerton Beauty' but will not grow so large in the garden. **HP**

'Trumpeter'
Reiter–USA 1946.
Another of the *F. triphylla* hybrids

'Tom Thumb' (see page 113)

with the group's characteristically long, tubular flowers produced in clusters. The colour of the blooms is pale geranium lake. The foliage is a bluish-green colour, and like the cultivar 'Mantilla' the growth is trailing. **B**

'Tuonela'
Blackwell–Britain 1970. Double
The tube and sepals are light pink and the corolla is long and a bluish-lavender shade with a hint of pink. The flowers are large, and the growth is strong and upright but will arch over under the weight of the blooms. **P**

'U.F.O.'
Handley–Britain 1972. Single
The tube and sepals are white and the sepals fold back tightly onto the pedicel. The corolla is a deep lilac colour and it opens flat, revealing a central patch of white. Medium sized flowers; upright growth. **P**

'Westminster Chimes'
Clyne–Britain 1976. Semi-double
A small-growing but freely flowering, very bushy plant. The sepals and tube are red and the corolla is a violet-blue colour. **P**

'White Pixie'
Merrist Wood–Britain 1968. Single
The tube and sepals are red, and the corolla white with red veins. The flowers are small and the leaves are light green in colour. Upright, bushy growth and very hardy. A sport from 'Pixie'. **HP**

'Westminster Chimes'

'White Spider'
Haag–USA 1951. Single
The flower is predominantly white but always lightly tinged with pink. The long sepals twist and reflex. The medium sized flowers are freely produced and the plant tends to grow horizontally. **SB**

'Winston Churchill'
Garson–USA 1942. Double
The tube and sepals are red. The full corolla is a deep lavender-blue but matures to a mauve-purple colour. The growth is upright, bushy and short jointed; the flowers are medium to large. This cultivar makes an excellent pot plant. **SP**

'W. P. Wood'
Wood–Britain 1954. Single
The tube and sepals are scarlet and the corolla is a violet-blue colour with a tinge of red at the base of the petals. Medium sized flowers; upright, bushy growth. An excellent hardy cultivar. **HP**

'Winston Churchill'

Tables of recommendations

Hardy species and cultivars for permanent bedding

Those plants marked with an star (★) can also be used as a hedging subject; the approximate maximum height that it is likely to attain in an area with only light frost in winter is given in brackets.

'Alice Hoffman'
'Blue Bush'
'Chillerton Beauty'★ (1 m, 3 ft)
'Drame'★ (1 m, 3 ft)
'Garden News'
'Lady Thumb'
'Lena'
'Madame Cornelissen'★ (1.25 m, 4 ft)
F. magellanica and varieties★ (3 m, 9 ft)
'Margaret'★ (1.25 m, 4 ft)
'Monsieur Thibaut'
'Mrs Popple'★ (1 m, 3 ft)
'Phenomenal'
'Phyllis'★ (1.25 m, 4 ft)
'Pixie'
'Prosperity'★ (0.6 m, 2 ft)
'Riccartonii'★ (1.75 m, 5 ft)
'Rose of Castile'
'Son of Thumb'
'Susan Travis'
'Tennessee Waltz'
'Tom Thumb'
'Trase'

Fuchsias for summer bedding

'Army Nurse'
'Autumnale'
'Brutus'
'Display'
'Hampshire Treasure'
'Kolding Perle'
'Strawberry Delight'
'Thalia'

Fuchsias suitable for growing as standards, pillars and pyramids

'Annabel'
'Checkerboard'
'Dark Eyes'
'Display'
'Marin Glow'
'Mrs Lovell Swisher'
'Peppermint Stick'
'Royal Velvet'
'Snowcap'
'Southgate'
'Spion Kop'
'Swingtime'
'Tennessee Waltz'

FUCHSIAS SUITABLE FOR HANGING BASKETS

'Cascade'
'Crackerjack'
'Eva Boerg'
'Golden Marinka'
'Harry Gray'
'La Campanella'
'Lakeside'
'Marinka'
'Red Spider'
'Sophisticated Lady'
'Swingtime'
'Trail Blazer'

FUCHSIAS SUITABLE FOR EXHIBITION

'Angela Leslie'
'Annabel'
'Derby Imp'
'Harry Gray'
'Iced Champagne'
'Leonora'
'Marin Glow'
'Marinka'
'Mieke Meursing'
'Mr A. Huggett'
'Nellie Nuttall'
'Plenty'
'Royal Velvet'
'Snowcap'
'Spion Kop'
'Swingtime'

Glossary

anther The pollen-bearing part at the tip of the stamen.

axil The point where a leaf joins the stem from which new growth or flowers emerge.

berry The fleshy fruit.

break To send out new growth. This can occur by pinching out the growing tip of a stem, or as the result of vigorous pruning of an old stem or of new growth produced at the end of the dormant season.

corolla A collective name for the petals of a flower.

cultivar A cultivated plant that has reached its present form through the intervention of man as distinct from a variety that occurs naturally in the wild. Abbreviated to cv.

dormancy A temporary state of rest that can be induced by withholding water for a period and by allowing the temperature to fall so that, in the case of a deciduous plant, the leaves fall. In the case of fuchsias, water must not be withheld completely, nor should the temperature be allowed to fall below freezing point or the plant will die.

epiphyte A plant that grows upon another plant. The roots grow in plant debris that collects in the forks of branches, etc. They use the host plant only as a means of support and are not parasites.

filament The stalk of an anther.

genus A group of species with common structural characteristics which are supposed to have derived from a common ancestor.

hybrid A plant produced by the crossing of two species or subspecies.

inflorescence The arrangement of flowers on the pedicel or flower stalk.

node The often slightly swollen point of origin of leaves on a stem.

ovary The female portion of a flower that contains embryonic seeds (ovules) which are fertilized by the pollen.

pedicel The stalk of an individual flower in an inflorescence.

peduncle The term is used for the stalk of a solitary flower or cluster of flowers.

petaloid In fuchsia terminology this usually refers to the small, poorly developed petals that occur round the base of the corolla of double-flowered forms. It can also apply to stamens that sometimes grow into flattened, petal-like forms.

pinch out To remove the growing tip of a stem using thumbnail and forefinger. The tip can also be cut out using a sharp knife or other instrument.

pistil The ovary, style and stigma.

Opposite:
'Trail Blazer' (see page 113)

pot back To shake old soil from a plant and to replant with fresh compost into a smaller pot. This process is often carried out at the start of a new growing season.

pot on To move the plant into a larger container with as little disturbance to the roots as possible.

re-pot To shake off old soil from the roots and replant with fresh compost into the same sized or larger pot. The terms re-pot and pot on have very different meanings and should not be confused.

sepal The outer part of the fuchsia flower bud that opens to reveal the corolla.

soft growth Young growth that has not yet hardened or matured.

species A group of plants that have essentially the same characteristics and are (or were) found in the wild and that come true from seed.

sport A mutation that occurs in a bud, which then develops to give a plant with a different coloured flower or perhaps variegated leaves. This mutation can arise spontaneously or be induced by artificial means.

stamen The filament and anther together.

stigma The enlarged sticky portion at the end of the style which receives the pollen.

stop To stop a stem is synonymous with pinching out.

style The stalk of the stigma, which connects it to the ovary.

tube The narrow, elongated section of the flower that joins the ovary to the sepals and corolla.

variety A distinct form of a species but of insufficient importance to justify it as a separate species or subspecies.

woody growth The older, woody or brown parts of the lower stems.

Acknowledgements

Line artwork by Howard Ryan

Photographs
Pat Brindley, pages 23, 58; Crown copyright © reproduced with the permission of the Controller, Her Majesty's Stationery Office, and the Director, Royal Botanic Gardens, Kew, pages 6, 12, 14, 40, 56; Jerry Harpur, pages 39 (Saling Hall), 43, 67; Photos Horticultural, pages 42, 71. The picture on page 77 is reproduced with the permission of The Royal Botanic Gardens, Kew.

All other photographs by David Clark, the author.

Taxonomy checked by Susyn Andrews, who works as a botanist at The Royal Botanic Gardens, Kew and is also a member of the Kew Magazine Editorial Committee. She studied amenity horticulture at The National Botanic Gardens, Glasnevin, Co. Dublin, Republic of Ireland.

Bibliography

The following publications are suitable for the amateur fuchsia grower.

Boullemier, L. B. *The Checklist of Species, Hybrids and Cultivars of the Genus Fuchsia.* Blandford Press, 1985. This is an authoritative list of descriptions gleaned from a multitude of sources. A unique and invaluable asset to the fuchsia enthusiast.
Clapham, S. *Fuchsias for House and Garden* David & Charles, 1982.
Clark, D. W. H. *The Oakleigh Guide to Fuchsias* Oakleigh Publications, 1985.
Ewart, R. *Fuchsia Lexicon* Blandford Press, 1982.
Proudly, B. & V. *Fuchsias in Colour* Blandford Press, 1975.
Saunders, E. *Wagtail's Book of Fuchsias.* Wagtail's Publications, Vol. 1, 1971; Vol. 2, 1972; Vol. 3, 1973. Beautifully produced coloured drawings and descriptions.
Walker, G. & A. *A Colour Guide to Fuchsias* Grange Publications, 1986.
Walker, G. & A. *A Second Colour Guide to Fuchsias* Grange Publications, 1986.
Wells, G. *Royal Horticultural Society Wisley Handbook. Fuchsias* Cassell, 1985.
Wilson, S. J. *Fuchsias* Faber & Faber, 1974.

The following is a list of papers of interest to botanists or the serious student of fuchsia history and nomenclature.

Berry, P. E. (1982) 'The Systematic and Evolution of *Fuchsia* section Fuchsia (Onagraceae)' *Annals of the Missouri Botanic Garden* 69, (1) 1–198.
Breedlove, D. E., Berry, P. E. & Raven, P. H. (1982) 'The Mexican and Central American Species of *Fuchsia* (Onagraceae) except for section Encliandra' *Annals of the Missouri Botanic Garden* 69, (1) 209–234.
Breedlove, D. E. (1969) 'The Systematics of *Fuchsia* section Encliandra (Onagraceae)' *University of California Publications in Botany* 53 1–69.
Munz, P. A. (1943) A Revision of the Genus *Fuchsia* (Onagraceae). *Proceedings of the California Academy of Natural Sciences* 25, (1) 1–138.
Wright, J. O. (1979) 'Fuchsia. A Garden History' *The Plantsman* 1 (3) 181–186.

Curtis's *Botanical Magazine* (now *The Kew Magazine*). This publication still maintains its long tradition of fine colour printing and articles on plants, plant collecting and conservation. Since it was established in 1787 nearly 10,500 colour plates have appeared by many of the best British botanical artists.

Index

Page numbers in italics indicate illustrations, d = line drawing